T0195858

A DRIVEN LIFE

How to Drive Yourself Into Serenity

RICHIE MANN

BALBOA.PRESS

A DIVISION OF HAY HOUSE

Balboa Press books may be ordered through booksellers or by contacting:

Balboa Press
A Division of Hay House
1663 Liberty Drive
Bloomington, IN 47403
www.balboapress.com
844-682-1282

Print information available on the last page.

ISBN: 979-8-7652-3010-7 (sc)
ISBN: 979-8-7652-3012-1 (hc)
ISBN: 979-8-7652-3011-4 (e)

Library of Congress Control Number: 2022911309

Balboa Press rev. date: 07/15/2022

Contents

Acknowledgments vii

Introduction ix

Chapter 1   The Inner Sanctum 1

Chapter 2   World War You 3

Chapter 3   Dashboard Intuition...6

Chapter 4   Is This Seat Taken?... 10

Chapter 5   When the Shift Hits the Fan............................ 15

Chapter 6   Guide Dance 19

Chapter 7   Accidentally On Purpose..................................22

Chapter 8   Road Is All the Rage..25

Chapter 9   Rebel with a Little Pause 30

Chapter 10 That's My Jam 33

Chapter 11 Clutter to the Gutter 38

Chapter 12 Fear-Wheel Drive.. 42

Chapter 13 Vehicle I.D. 46

Chapter 14 Misery Loves Company.................................... 51

Chapter 15 Controlling Disinterest....................................56

Chapter 16 Parking Spot On... 61

Chapter 17 Changing Lanes in Vain 64

Chapter 18 Back in the U.S.S. Car.................................... 69

Chapter 19 The Invisible Man 74

Chapter 20 The I of the Storm...79
Chapter 21 Oh! Kla Home A...83
Chapter 22 It's Not Personal; It's Personal.........................88
Chapter 23 Give Me a Sign...92
Chapter 24 Life Can Be Fogged Up.....................................99
Chapter 25 Phone-y Behavior..102
Chapter 26 DUI or Don't I?..105

Conclusion 109
Angry Driver Checklist...111

Acknowledgments

There are so many people who deserve credit for inspiring this book. First and foremost, I would like to thank my codriver and sometimes navigator, Cynthia Bunch Cornacchio. We have traveled down many highways and byways together. We've had our share of collisions, wrong turns, and getting lost in the middle of nowhere. We've also traveled to so many sacred and amazing places together and shared a ton of laughter, tears of sadness or joy, and miracles. So many miracles. We've traveled separately at times in different vehicles, miles apart and in opposite directions, but we have always managed to somehow end up on the same road together. Next, I'd like to thank my three angels, Dyan, Caity, and Sarah, who started out as passengers in my vehicle and quickly turned into drivers and navigators, showing me so many different and better ways to travel the many roads of life. The driving students become the driving instructors! Thank you, Mom and Dad, for bringing me into this world. I know I didn't always drive down the roads you would have liked me to, but you still let me make my own way, in my own vehicle, and learn from my own wrong turns.

Thanks to my big sister Roe for her gifts that ignited my love of reading and writing.

Thanks to Marvin and Madeline Bunch for treating me like a son. "Bless yourself!"

Thank you to Moses Starr Jr., Anita Little Raven Starr, Betty Hart, and my entire Cheyenne-Arapaho Tribe of Oklahoma family for teaching me that there are many different roads that all eventually lead to the same destination. It is my honor that all of you have chosen to share the ride with me.

Thank you to Tom Hatzel for seeing something in this book and encouraging me to actually turn it from a dream into reality.

Thank you to Andrew Caffrey for his brilliant legal mind.

Thank you to Leslie Baltes for pointing out some very crucial road signs along the way.

Thank you to Mike "Sarge" McPartland for being my partner in comedy for all of these years.

Thank you Jill and Ted for reading the roughs.

Hearfelt thanks to April and Darryl, for their input and encouragement.

If I missed anyone (I am sure that I did), I am truly sorry, and I thank you as well. Thanks also to my Higher Power for sending me the words to write and the vehicle to drive. I love you all.

Introduction

This book has been floating around in my head for a very long time. I had to get it down the very long road to my heart before I could actually write it.

It started out one day when I was driving on the New York State Thruway listening to an audiobook of *The Seat of the Soul* by Gary Zukav.

I was at a very calming and deep part of the book when all of a sudden another car cut into my lane, almost colliding with my car. I went absolutely bat-crap crazy in the blink of an eye. I began cursing and tailgating the other vehicle. I tried cutting the other car off, and when it finally began exiting the thruway, I pulled up alongside and gave the other driver my middle finger along with a very explicit profanity-laced rant. I can only imagine how insane I must have looked through the windows of both of our cars as I gestured and yelled like a lunatic. As I continued driving, I settled right back in to listening to the audiobook and resumed learning how to be a kinder, gentler soul, but with a little less conviction than I had previously felt.

That night as I lay in bed reflecting on the day's events, I could still feel the lingering resentment toward the other driver. I still felt the anger that had exploded inside of me in that instant. I traced the resentment back and realized I was already in a go-to-war mood when I woke up that morning, and I had started listening to the audiobook to get myself out of that mood. It also dawned on me that I was using that other driver as an outlet for my pent-up frustration. I began thinking about how many times I got angry when driving, how many different driving situations triggered my anger, and all of the different ways I expressed my anger. I had enough ideas to write a book!

This book is a drive down my emotional highway. It is not meant to preach. It is meant to be identified with. Hopefully if you do identify with any part of it, you will be able to laugh a little and maybe learn something about yourself.

Now here's the part where I'm supposed to say you are reading this book at this moment in time because you are meant to be reading it. It was written just for you, and it was just waiting for the right moment for you to find it. Maybe so. Whatever. I'm just glad you found it (or maybe it found you) and that you are reading it. I hope you have as much fun reading it as I did writing it. See you on the road. Hopefully we won't be giving each other the finger!

THE INNER SANCTUM

Every day, I arise, say my prayers, meditate, take a shower, and get dressed.

I put on my underwear and socks. I put on my pants, then my shirt, and then whatever footwear I have chosen for the day.

I also wrap myself in a couple of thousand pounds or more of steel, plastic, rubber, vinyl, chrome, and glass and head out into the world.

I believe this wrapping makes me invincible to all that is going on around me. I believe this wrapping gives me the protection to abandon all of the decent principles I have been taught and believe in.

This wrapping, which is more commonly known as a car, truck, SUV, crossover, minivan, tractor trailer, bus, pickup, or hybrid, becomes a sanctuary. It is impenetrable to all, with the exception of those whom I deign worthy enough to enter its sacred space. It is my mobile fortress where I alone am allowed to touch its steering wheel and pedals—where only I am allowed to adjust the temperature and fiddle lovingly with the 223-satellite radio/CD/AM/FM/Bluetooth buttons like a madman, searching out the perfect soundtrack or commentary for my journey.

Let no one dare to adjust one degree of the temperature or touch the coveted audio controls without first asking my permission, lest they be banished to the barren back-seat realm, never to be heard from again. (There are exceptions; we will get to back-seat drivers later on in the book.)

As I turn the key and hear the engine fire up, I am assured that all is right in my world and no one or nothing will block my way as I venture out onto the road ahead. Not one person or thing will interfere with me reaching wherever it is I am going.

Let the journey begin.

Suggestion: For one day, try letting your passenger pick the station or songs in the car. Let your passengers adjust the climate in the vehicle to their preference. Don't make any comment whatsoever. See how long you can do this until you hit the imaginary eject-passenger button on the dashboard.

2

WORLD WAR YOU

I love the term "defensive driving." It's very apropos.

It implies war, at least in my mind. It also suggests that, in order to have defensive driving, there must be a flip side of that coin—offensive driving.

I'm going to get in my car and defend myself against all of those other drivers who woke up today and decided they were going to be doing some offensive driving against me.

So what, in my mind, does defensive driving consist of?

It means I am protecting myself from the actions of other drivers—the drivers who cut me off suddenly or squeeze into the safe space I have left between my car and the vehicle in front of me, or the drivers who may not see that stop sign or red light because they are busy reading that very important text or email that just can't wait until they are not controlling a potentially lethal weapon at a high rate of speed. I could go on, but I'm sure you get where I am going with this. (If you don't, you might want to get out your GPS and program Pretty Obvious Boulevard into it.)

Some days I might decide to play offense.

I'll get into my car with the intention of offending every driver on the road. I will refuse to signal before changing lanes or turning. I will make sure I cut into whatever lane I want on a moment's notice, causing the other drivers to swerve angrily. I will tailgate other vehicles even though they are going fifteen miles per hour over the speed limit in the center lane. I will slow down even more or hit my brakes suddenly to piss off the idiot who is tailgating me. I will drive twenty miles per hour or sixty miles per hour on a single-lane road even though the speed limit is forty miles per hour. I will speed up just enough to not let you in even though you put your signal on to move over into my lane. I will slow down just enough to not let you get around me or the car that has you boxed in on the other side. I will speed up just enough for myself to go through the yellow light but not enough for you to make it through. Make no mistake—I will drive offensively, whether it be consciously or not.

Does this reflect the way I am living my life? Yes, of course it does.

Every day I am faced with the choice of living defensively or offensively, but guess what I have discovered? Ready for some good news? I have discovered there is a third choice! I do not have to be defensive or offensive. I can just be. No matter what the other drivers are doing, I do not have to react any way at all. I can just stay on the road and let whatever is happening be. Just be and let it be. I will get to where I am going all the same, and I will not be affected by the other drivers' choices. What a concept! By not reacting to the other drivers, I become. What do I become? I become nothing. I am neither defending nor offending. I am just being. The illusions on the road of life become just that—illusions. The windshield becomes crystal clear the moment I drop being defensive or offensive and just be.

"Be what?" you ask. That's it! Just be. In that one instant of just being, everything else on the road becomes a blur, and the road ahead and the road behind become meaningless. The journey and the destination become one. I've already arrived. I just don't know it, yet I do know it.

So go ahead and have at it. Do your best or your worst because this driver will not be participating in the Vehicle World War today.

Well, maybe just until some inconsiderate butt-munch cuts me off. I am, after all, only human.

Suggestion: Make a list of all of the things other drivers do that really rattle your cage. Write down the emotion it brings up for you.

Next to the offense, write down what you fantasize about doing to that other driver or their vehicle.

Example: Driver cut me off even though I was going seventy-five miles per hour in the left lane. Anger; frustration. Would love to ram them from behind and cause them to crash.

Bring the list to your local police station or psych center and see how they react. Fun times!

DASHBOARD INTUITION

Here's a fun fact you might not know: the little warning indicators on your instrument panel that light up when your oil is low or wiper fluid needs to be changed or tire pressure is low are nicknamed "idiot lights." True story!

I'm guessing it's because the car manufacturers believe only an idiot would need a light to tell them when something is wrong with their car. Maybe they think that only an idiot would let something on their car get so bad for so long that it gets to the point where the car itself is screaming out in pain.

It could also be because some people will continue to drive for many days or weeks or years with one of those lights on. I carpooled with a guy who drove with his check engine light on for almost a year. The only reason he got it taken care of was that his car was due for state inspection, and he needed to renew his registration. Otherwise, he would have driven that vehicle until the motor was a pile of rusting junk, hanging on by hoses and wires and being dragged behind him like an anchor. Idiotic behavior, some would say.

Whatever the reason, I think it's a pretty funny name.

I believe that as human beings we also have idiot lights. (No, I don't mean those lights that go off in our heads when someone who we think is an idiot is approaching us.)

I'm talking about that feeling that we get in our guts when something is not quite right.

Or that hunch we have that something is about to happen that might not be in our best interest.

I'm going to use the *e* word here—emotions.

Our emotions are our warning lights. Our fear-based feelings, such as anger, sadness, jealousy, depression, etc., are all warning lights telling us something is off in our drivetrain or motor and needs to be taken care of.

Unlike our vehicles, we do not come with a manufacturer's manual to look up what light is related to what problem in the vehicle's system.

We do not have mechanics and technicians who can diagnose and repair our broken or worn-out parts or troubleshoot our malfunctioning systems.

Or do we?

Great news! We do!

Our manuals come in many different forms, written by many different people, but they all come from the same source, and it's not General Motors! You can choose to call the source whatever you'd like, and you may not even believe that there is a source, but that's irrelevant in this instance.

Our mechanics and technicians are our medical doctors and our therapists. They are our spiritual teachers and guides. They are the leaders of whatever houses of worship we choose to find comfort in. Sometimes they are the people who are closest to us. They can see something going on in us that maybe we just can't see for ourselves. But ultimately, what it all comes down to is this: we don't need to know anything else except one basic concept—love.

Love is the tool that turns off all of the idiot lights.

Love is the socket wrench that will tighten any loose bolts. Love is the quart of clean oil that will lubricate all of those stuck parts.

Love is the patch that will help that flat tire to reinflate and hold air again.

Fear is like sand in a gas tank or a loose belt or a flat tire. Your vehicle cannot move forward if any of these conditions exist, and just like those gauges and warning lights are there to tell you when something is wrong with the vehicle, your emotions are there to light up your warning lights when something is wrong in your system.

Question: how many times have you ignored or not even noticed your vehicle's warning lights when they were on?

If you're like me, too many times to count on both hands.

When I think of all the times I have not paid attention to my warning lights and gauges, it becomes quite clear to me that I have ended up in a ditch, or stuck on the side of the road in the middle of nowhere, or, worst case, causing a major crash with many others involved and with injuries of all sorts to myself and to them.

All of these scenarios could have been avoided had I just paid attention to those idiot lights.

Suggestion: Take some time to read some of the "manufacturer's manuals" that are out there.

Find comfort in your spiritual beliefs and in whatever higher power you feel called to.

Change your oil when it needs to be changed, and never try to drive on a flat tire. You'll only wind up with a bent rim and a useless tire.

Pay attention to your idiot lights!

IS THIS SEAT TAKEN?

Driver or passenger?

A funny thing happened the other night.

I was a passenger in my friend's vehicle. As we were driving through town on a one-lane road, another vehicle came up from behind us on the right (which was in this case on the *wrong* side because he was driving where there was no actual lane) and cut off us and the other two vehicles ahead of us.

My friend went ballistic, cursing and banging the steering wheel and yelling, "Can you believe this crap?"

I, on the other hand, remained pretty calm and didn't really even think much of it except that the person driving was pretty inconsiderate of others, and where was a cop when you needed one?

My buddy continued to carry on for a good five minutes or so, and I just let him vent. I certainly understood how he was feeling, and I was wondering why I just did not feel the same way as he did at that moment in time.

That night when I was lying in bed, I thought about it.

I realized that the reason that I was not upset was because even though we were both in the same vehicle, in the exact same situation, I wasn't driving. Someone else was, and that allowed me to not take the situation personally. I did not have my hands on the wheel, and I was not in control. I was once removed, and that made it easier for me to detach from what was happening at the time.

What a concept!

If I let someone else drive, I immediately see things from a different perspective, and I don't take what's happening in the vehicle so personally.

Seems to me like it's all about control.

I live my everyday life much the same way.

When I believe I am at the wheel of my life—speeding through red lights, or getting lost on some back road in the middle of nowhere, or cutting people off to get somewhere two minutes sooner—how does my life look?

It looks pretty much like one of those cartoon maps where you see the dotted line traveling in crazy zigzags and circles to get to the X that could have taken one straight line to get to.

It *feels* like that too. Chaotic. Lost. Going nowhere fast.

It seems like even though I am at the wheel, I have lost control and gone off the road I'm meant to be on. It's not a good feeling.

So maybe the answer is to let someone else drive—someone who knows every inch of the road. Someone who has planned the route carefully. Someone who does not speed through red lights or get lost on back roads, or cut people off to arrive somewhere two minutes sooner. Who is this mysterious driver?

Only you can answer that one for yourself.

Your road may be on a completely different part of the planet from mine. It may be all highways and parkways. It may be side streets and back roads. It may be a combination of all different types of roads and streets and avenues.

It may have some detours. It may have some unpaved stretches. It may be well lit at times and dark and foreboding at other times.

My driver knows everything about every road I've just mentioned and everything about every road I may have left out.

My driver knows all of the roads eventually lead to the same destination.

My driver knows every road goes exactly where it should go even though it might not seem like it when I am on it.

My driver knows that as a passenger I might think we are on the wrong road at times.

My driver knows that as a passenger I might have to stop and stretch my legs and use the bathroom every so often.

My driver knows sometimes I may think I should be driving because my driver is not going as fast or as slow as I want, or stopping at the world's biggest frying pan that I always wanted to see, or avoiding all of that city traffic at the height of rush hour.

Yet my driver still keeps driving. On and on. Until we get where we are going.

As a passenger, I get to enjoy the scenery a lot more than if I was driving. I get to lie down on the back seat and take a nap like when I was a little kid on a long ride home.

As a passenger, I don't have to keep checking the rearview mirror.

As a passenger, I can sit back and enjoy the ride a little bit more.

Of course, as a passenger I'm still in the vehicle experiencing everything the driver is experiencing.

I'm just experiencing it with a different outlook and attitude than if I was driving.

Guess what?

Sometimes my driver lets me pick the soundtrack.

But only if I promise to wear my seatbelt.

Suggestion: The next time you feel angry while driving, try to think like a passenger.

See if you can not take whatever the other drivers are doing as a personal attack against you. After all, when you got behind the wheel, did you have someone specifically in mind who you were going to cut off or tailgate? (If you did, please seek immediate psychiatric attention.) What makes you think someone else did?

Check out how different your intentions can be as a driver or as a passenger and what the differences are. I think you'll be surprised.

WHEN THE SHIFT HITS THE FAN

There are basically two different types of transmissions in a vehicle—manual or automatic.

A manual transmission, or stick, requires a lot more work than an automatic transmission. Some drivers prefer a manual transmission because they say it takes more concentration and therefore connects them more to the road. I drive both types, and I'd just like to say there is some degree of truth to that—but shouldn't I be concentrating on and connecting to the road no matter what I'm driving? Being responsible for careening around in a potentially lethal weapon deserves all of my concentration and connection as far as I'm concerned, but I digress.

So, a stick requires that one must change gears manually by pressing in a clutch with their foot and shifting the gear lever to the next position. It does take some coordination and timing to move the vehicle without it bucking and lurching or even stalling out completely. There is a rhythm to pressing in the clutch pedal and shifting gears and then releasing the clutch while giving the car more gas. It's definitely harder than driving an automatic, but it is also strangely empowering. (At least to me it is.)

After years of practice, I hardly ever buck or stall out like I used to when my wife took me out in her 1969 VW Beetle to teach me how to "drive a stick."

I'll never forget being in a line of traffic on a hill waiting for the light to turn green. I was in a state of silent panic because I knew the car would drift backward into the car behind me if I didn't quickly give it enough gas as I released the clutch. It could have even stalled out, and that would've been a disaster as well.

I gave it too much gas, and the car lurched forward, but at least I didn't roll back and hit the car behind me.

I was so embarrassed and frustrated, and I almost gave up trying to learn after that experience, but my wife assured me that with practice, hill climbing would eventually become second nature—kind of like everyday life. The more I practice certain things, positive or negative, the more they become second nature.

Which do I choose to give more gas to? Which one will take me forward up or backward down the hill?

Captain Obvious, do you care to answer this one?

Automatic transmissions do all of the shifting for the driver. All the driver has to do is steer and brake (which is still a huge responsibility). It's a completely different experience from driving a stick shift, but it will get you to the same destination.

Both transmissions move you forward, and both have a reverse gear as well.

Driving in reverse is much more difficult than driving forward (unless you are a professional driver or just have a natural ability to travel backward).

You have to turn the steering wheel left to go right, and you have to use your mirrors or rotate your neck like that kid in *The Exorcist* to see where you're headed.

Life is like that too. No, not like *The Exorcist,* although I do feel like I am possessed by demons at times, but that's a whole 'nother book.

Life is much harder to live in reverse. When I'm constantly looking in my rearview mirror or turning the wheel left to go right, my life feels so much more difficult. When I live life in the past, it takes me that much longer to get to the present.

Living in the past is much different from remembering the past and learning from my experiences. One serves no purpose and prevents me from moving forward while the other allows me to remember certain routes that I may or may not want to take again.

Checking the rearview mirror obsessively can cause me not to focus on what is happening directly ahead on the road in front of me, and I could wind up plowing into that tractor trailer that suddenly stopped short.

Checking my rearview mirror responsibly will allow me to be aware of what is happening behind me while concentrating fully on what is unfolding directly in front of me. That's a much safer way to drive.

Suggestion: Try to remember that your rearview mirror, like your past, is simply a reflection of things that are going on behind you. If you are moving forward, you are moving away from those things, and there is nothing you can do to change them. I once heard someone say that the rearview mirror is much smaller than the windshield for a reason. Knowing where you have been can help you get to where you are going, but to go back you have to go backward, and life, at least to me, is about moving forward.

Whatever type of transmission you are driving with, remember that driving in reverse is always more difficult than driving forward.

It's impossible to drive safely if you keep your eyes focused on the rearview mirror, so keep your attention on the road around you and ahead of you (though not too far ahead).

6

GUIDE DANCE

GPS. What does it stand for?

Gets People Somewhere?

Get Pissed at Something?

Gives Positive Support?

It actually stands for Global Positioning System.

Pretty intense, right? GPS can tell you exactly where you are anywhere on the planet as long as you can get a signal to and from a satellite. You also have to be in a country where the names of places and streets and avenues and towns have been programmed into whatever system you are using. It's not 100 percent reliable 100 percent of the time, but it still can be an incredibly useful and helpful tool to get you where you need to go.

My cellular phone is my GPS, so I can even use it when I'm not behind the wheel. No more "I couldn't find it, I got lost" excuses for this guy!

I can't keep track of how many places my GPS has taken me, although it didn't always take me to them the quickest or most logical way.

I have had many arguments with my GPS when it has taken me a roundabout way or kept increasing the time it was going to take to arrive at my destination. Some of those arguments have been quite loud and profane with me calling her (my GPS has a woman's voice) every nasty name I can think of. Funny thing is the arguments always seem to be one sided. My GPS never reacts. She just keeps on speaking in her calm monotone, no matter how frustrated or loud or angry I become with her.

She is also still willing to give me directions even though I have not been nice to her.

What a beautiful lesson in detachment.

If only I could be that detached when someone is yelling at me or being nasty or angry (real or imagined on my part). Imagine still sending that person love and forgiveness right in that moment, like my GPS does by sending me in the right direction despite my attempts to go off of the path. I wonder how that would change the situation for me. I wonder how that would change my entire life for me.

Now you may be saying to yourself, "Self, I think this guy has really gone in a ditch on this one. He's using an inanimate object as an example of human behavior!"

But I am going to invoke poetic license in this case because, number one, it's my book and I can do whatever the frick I want to, and number two, the GPS was programmed at some point by a human, so it comes close enough.

Suggestion: Try detaching calmly when you think the GPS has sent you into another dimension rather than guiding you to Brooklyn, and see how much faster you will get back on track. Then try detaching calmly the next time you feel you are under attack or feeling put-upon or rejected by someone. See how fast you can get yourself back on track. See if you can find a way to forgive the person(s) or yourself. See if you can find something positive in what may seem like a negative situation.

GPS=Good Positive Self.

ACCIDENTALLY ON PURPOSE

Accidents! (Or are they?)

I have had my share of collisions, fender benders, and bumps and dings over my illustrious driving career. (No, not since the wheel was invented, wiseass. I'm not quite that old!)

Some were directly my fault, some were not, and some were a combination of faults.

The one common denominator in all these incidents was (drumroll) … me!

What, you might ask, could my part be in an accident if I was hit from behind by a guy on his cell phone whilst innocently slowing down my car as the car ahead of me pulled off of the road?

Easy. I was there. That's it. I was there at that moment to provide a target for this careless jerk to plow into. (Detachment would be a great thing right here, wouldn't it?)

I did nothing wrong, yet my car was totaled, and I was hugely inconvenienced as I went through insurance and rental-car hell.

How is that fair? It's not. Or is it?

That's the mystery of life and the wonder of the universe. We never get the full story no matter who is doing what to whom.

We never get to see the end until it's the end, and then who knows if the means to the end was just a beginning of a new start? (Wow, I am really new-aging it up here! I must be a spiritual guy!)

Anyway, I have been the cause of someone else's grief a few times myself. I caused a collision once in Manhattan, and the police said it was clearly my fault. It was. The other driver did nothing wrong, and I was completely in the wrong. It was a mistake on my part, and I had to face the consequences of my error in judgement. Thank goodness for insurance! That's what insurance is for. (Everyone has said that at least once in their lives!) So that time my part was very clear to me. See? Personal responsibility.

Guess what? In some way, I am always personally responsible for what my life looks like at any given moment. I might not always know in what way, but I don't have to.

All I have to know is that there was an accident, and I was involved in it. Now what do I do next?

My degree of responsibility will determine my degree of consequences. Plain and simple. The universe is always fair and loving and compassionate. It is also impartial. Cause in, effect out. Every minute, every hour, every day, and on and on and on.

So now I look at accidents as incidents, and I try to see what my part in the incident is and take it from there. Sometimes it is not easy to see my part, and sometimes it is.

Suggestion: The next time you are involved in an incident that you feel you didn't cause, look harder and deeper. Try to see what your part is, no matter how small.

Then do whatever must be done to continue moving forward, no matter who was at fault.

Forgive yourself if it was you. Forgive the other driver if it was them—no matter what the circumstances. I know when I practice forgiveness, I always feel better about myself. It's amazing how other people seem to be better people when I am doing the best I can do. Is that accidental? I think not!

It's all a matter of what I think eventually will manifest in some way, shape, or form. So I try to keep my thoughts positive. With practice, positive thinking becomes habit, and then I have less and less to forgive others and myself for because I do not negatively judge them or myself.

8

ROAD IS ALL THE RAGE

Road rage.

This is where the rubber hits the road. This is the heart of what this book is about.

Where does it come from? Why does it always seem to happen no matter how great a mood I am in before I put the key in the ignition?

I believe it's because my rage is already there, bubbling beneath the surface. Driving just presents so many situations that give my rage an opportunity to boil over.

There are so many things I can't control:

Getting cut off.

Being tailgated even though I'm not driving too slowly.

The car in front of me changing lanes without signaling.

The person in front of me in the left lane going ten miles per hour under the speed limit.

Another driver texting or talking on their cell phone.

That car that goes really slowly in front of me then speeds up just enough for them to go through the yellow light but leaving me slamming on my brakes to not go through the red light.

A drunk or drugged-up driver.

Someone cutting me off in a parking lot to grab that space I was just about to pull into.

The list goes on and on. Any or all of these things can set me off in a tenth of a second. I can go from sunny and pleasant to a Category 5 hurricane in the blink of an eye.

Why?

As I stated previously, I believe it's already there in me. For me, it's all about lack of control. The feeling that I am not in control of a situation will always tap into my reserve of anger. The feelings of being subservient or abandoned or not loved just pop right up.

How can these other drivers not see me or care about me?

Don't they know how I feel?

Can't they see who I am?

Do they think I am powerless or weak?

How dare they ignore me!

I matter, and they can't seem to get that through their thick skulls.

Why are they so uncaring and inconsiderate of my feelings?

All of these thoughts and feelings happen in a matter of seconds, yet they can take hours to dissipate. That's because they are already there. Driving just gives them an opportunity to surface.

I recall a time when my partner and I and our three daughters were driving on the Major Deegan Expressway. It was nighttime, and the car in front of us was driving extremely slowly. We were in the middle of having a pleasant time with the girls, singing along to a CD, and my partner turned to me and said, "Hit him with the brights!" I thought this was an excellent idea, so I starting flashing my high beams at him or her. We started chanting, "Hit 'em with the brights!" in time with the music while I shone my high beams into their rearview mirror until they finally moved over. We all cheered like we had just scored the winning run.

Reflecting back, I can see how my partner's simple suggestion quickly escalated into an aggressive group energy that could have ended with someone being harmed. The next day, my partner explained to the girls that what we had done was not appropriate behavior, and we never did that again. (Well, that particular behavior anyway. Hey, that's why I am writing this book!)

So what is the best way to solve this dilemma?

There are a few things I can do. Hitting the pause button is a big one. When I feel that anger start to boil up, it helps to have a positive affirmation, prayer, poem, or song to say to myself. Usually in the time it takes to say whatever it is I say to myself, the anger will subside.

Sometimes a few seconds of silent pausing works. Letting my mind go blank for a moment or two (okay, I know there are many of you who know me who will say that this isn't much of a stretch) will help. The silence will sometimes shake the anger from my mind.

Reversing roles can help too. For example, when have I not cut someone off or tailgated or not let someone get in front of me? Did I think of others in those moments? Maybe I should empathize instead of criticize.

I also try not to take the other driver's actions so personally anymore. *Try* is the keyword here because as much as I'd like to say that I always do, I don't always succeed. So I try my best. That's all I can do sometimes.

Suggestion: When another driver pushes your buttons, take a pause and ask yourself if it's really a big deal. Ask yourself if you really and truly believe the other driver set out that day to stick it to you personally. Think of how ridiculous and unlikely that really is. You really have no way of knowing if they truly did, but tell yourself that of course they didn't (because odds are that they didn't!).

By the time you do that, the other driver will be just another person behind the wheel of a vehicle, just like you. Ask yourself, did you set out to piss off another driver when you turned the key in the ignition?

Give others the same leeway you would like given to you. We don't know what type of day or moment or life someone else is having in that other vehicle.

They could be ill.

They could have suffered the loss of a loved one.

They might have just gotten laid off from their job.

They might be in the middle of a relationship breaking up.

They might have that same rage so many of us have bubbling beneath the surface.

Try to let it ride and let it go.

I guarantee if you practice letting go, it might just help you to feel better (about yourself and others).

9

REBEL WITH A LITTLE PAUSE

Rules of the road.

Let me start by saying I would never and have never parked in a handicapped space. Okay, now that that's out of the way, I can start this hypothetical chapter.

I don't know if I should be admitting this in public, but I have broken the law. I am an outlaw. A rebel. A societal nonconformist.

I have coasted through a stop sign.

I have driven through a red light.

I have driven over the speed limit.

I have tailgated another vehicle.

I have turned right on red in a no-turning-right-on-red zone.

I'm sure I've done more, but you get my drift, and I'm sure you understand this is all hypothetical. (I can't mention that enough.)

It's funny because I think I'm a pretty law-abiding citizen otherwise, but wrap a car around me and all bets are off.

I often wonder why I think I'm not really doing anything wrong when I'm clearly disobeying very unambiguous laws.

Let's face it. The sign says "SPEED LIMIT" or "STOP" or "DO NOT ENTER," but I still look both ways to check for the local constabulary. Then if the coast is clear, I go ahead and break that law. (Hypothetically!)

Most of the time, I don't even feel a twinge of guilt. I just feel a sense of getting away with something I shouldn't have. Screw the man! Nobody is going to tell me when and where I should stop or turn or slow down! (Of course these are just thoughts I never, ever act on!)

Uh-oh! I think I see red and blue lights coming up behind me! Gotta go!

Suggestion: I know I have that "everyone does it so it's no big deal" attitude about breaking the rules of driving, and if you feel you do too, then take a look at why you feel the rules don't apply to you.

I'll bet you aren't a shoplifter. (If you are, I really hope you didn't shoplift this book, although I would be kinda flattered.)

I'll bet you aren't a burglar. (Put this book back on that coffee table right now!)

So why are you an outlaw behind the wheel? I actually have no idea! Do I look like a mind reader to you? I know why I am! It's because I want to feel like I am calling the shots. I am in control. I am unique. I am special. There are so few things I can control when it comes to the government and the law that I feel that breaking a minor law that "everybody else breaks too" gives me some kind of control. Imagine if everyone at a four-way-stop intersection decided to bend the law at the same time. It's not a pretty picture. I always have to keep in mind that my taking control of certain things might not always be in the interest of the greater good.

To find out your answers, please see a therapist (and maybe bring along an extra copy of this book to read together!) because I am certainly not qualified to analyze anyone but myself, and I'm pretty certain I'm not really even qualified to do that.

But, I do know my own truth, and I do know when I'm not telling it to myself. I have to always be honest with myself, and following the rules of traffic is a great way to see if I really am.

10

THAT'S MY JAM

Traffic jam.

There's nothing like a little togetherness. People gathered for a common cause. Sharing. Caring. Cooperating. There is strength in numbers. United we stand, divided we fall. All for one, and one for all! Do unto others as we would have them do unto us.

Until we are all sitting in our cars in the middle of a traffic jam. Goodbye sharing. So long caring. See you later cooperating. All bets are off.

I can't think of many other things that have tried my patience more than sitting on the Long Island Expressway during rush hour and having it take forty-five minutes to go three miles.

Where are all of you coming from? Where are all of you going? Why did you all leave at the same time? Don't you know that I have somewhere to be? What the hell is wrong wit youse?

Here are some thoughts that go through my head:

"Oh wait, there goes one idiot trying to squeeze between two cars that are going 3 miles per hour because he's tired of going 2 miles per hour. He's not even signaling—just forcing his way in like there are no other cars there."

"There goes someone else not letting someone get over so they can get off at their exit."

"Someone else is driving on the shoulder and then cutting in at the last minute. What a jerk!"

Horns start blaring. Tempers start flaring. What happened to sharing, caring, and cooperating? Look in your rearview mirror! They've all been run over like a squirrel trying unsuccessfully to make it across the road.

I've cursed at the top of my lungs, banged on the steering wheel until my hands hurt, and thumped my head against the back of my seat until it feels like a ripe watermelon. Guess what? None of that stuff helps.

It's all angry, negative energy, and it's got nowhere to go. It's trapped in the car right there with me. It's churning in my solar plexus and swirling around in my head, and it makes me disoriented and hurts like hell. It's like a personal tornado ring right there in my vehicle—all destruction and mayhem.

So what can I do about it?

I can pray.

I can play a game in my head.

I can think of all of the things in my life I have to be grateful for.

I can listen to music and sing along at the top of my lungs.

I can listen to music and sing along quietly.

I can listen to music and not sing along at all. (There are such things as instrumentals.)

I can listen to an audiobook (hint hint!).

I can take that beautiful calming pause as many times as I need to.

I can remember that none of what is happening around me is personally directed at me.

I can try to think of new ways to cope besides the ones that I have just mentioned.

Guess what?

I am going to get to where I am going eventually.

I may be late, and I may be tired, but I will get there.

If I am really practicing the principles of positive thinking and using the coping strategies I have learned, I will not only get there, but I will get there much less frustrated and emotionally exhausted then if I were just letting the tornado wreak its unbridled havoc.

Now sometimes traffic is beyond our control. If I have to commute during peak traffic times, then there's nothing I can really do about that. But if I have an hour to be somewhere and I give myself fifty-nine minutes, whose responsibility is that? Especially if I know the traffic patterns of my route. But, traffic happens at all different times and for all different reasons, so it's never really in my control.

That means I have to have a certain amount of acceptance when I am on a journey.

Kind of like my life.

I never know when traffic is going to block my way in life.

Do I bang my head on life's steering wheel, or do I look for positive ways to deal with life's traffic?

It's obvious which way would lead to a calmer, more peaceful life, but sometimes I just want what I want when I want it. The universe is like an endless highway, and highways don't really go by what I want when I want it.

They just are there. Highways don't create the traffic, yet I blame them and curse them and don't accept the traffic on them. I also have a tendency to forget I am a part of the traffic. I am creating it along with all of the other vehicles.

Much like my life in this universe.

If I go with the flow, whether fast or slow, I'll continue to grow.

Patience. Acceptance. Tolerance. Humility. *Path*.

If I practice these concepts when traffic is at its worst, they will stay with me when the road ahead is wide open. The journey becomes much more important than the destination. I arrive when I arrive. (Try not to have this "arrive when I arrive" philosophy if you have set work hours and you are commuting to your job and you've given yourself fifty-nine minutes for an hour commute!)

I become a calmer, softer human. I see I am creating traffic along with all of the other drivers even though I can only be responsible for driving *my* car. Just like my life. I am only responsible for my life. I cannot live anyone else's life. However, just like being a contributor to the traffic that affects others, what I do affects others, so I have to remember to choose wisely and with consideration rather than ignorantly and selfishly.

Welcome home. Welcome home. Welcome home.

Suggestion: Try to turn traffic into a learning experience rather than a tortuous nightmare. I know it's hard to do, but try.

Consciously try to shift your thinking (pun intended) from negative thoughts to positive thoughts.

Be grateful you have a vehicle to be stuck in traffic in. Be grateful you have somewhere to go. Be grateful you can choose whether to react negatively or respond positively when you feel you are stuck somehow on your life's journey. Your thinking will change your direction and get you unstuck if you allow it to.

Try to remember you can only be behind the wheel of the vehicle *you* are driving. Let the other drivers be responsible for their vehicles, forgive them if they are not as responsible as you are, and forgive yourself if you are not as responsible as they are.

And lay off of that horn!

11

CLUTTER TO THE GUTTER

What's in the trunk (or *boot* for my UK readers)?

What's in the center console?

What's in the glove compartment?

The other day, I was looking for my registration. I opened my glove compartment, and inside was a screwdriver, some CDs, the owner's manual, an expired insurance card, and one glove.

I opened the center console and found six pens, four of which didn't write anymore; an electric bill from a year ago; some mints, both wrapped and unwrapped (which left a sticky mess on the bill and the pens); and a Swiss Army knife.

Various receipts from supermarkets and big box stores. More CDs. Half a roll of electrical tape. Some pennies. Hair ties. An empty dental floss container. Another glove (that didn't match the one in the glove compartment). Four toothpicks.

Some bolts. A random piece of plastic. A hair brush with hair in it. Yuck!

Needless to say, I was pretty frustrated by the time I found the registration at the bottom of the pile. I figured I may as well clean it all out, and at the same time take a look under the seats, in the seat pockets, and in the trunk. Lo and behold (I've always wanted to say that but never had the right opportunity until now), I found messes and chaos in all of those areas as well.

I grabbed a trash bag, sorted through the piles of stuff, threw out the trash, kept the good stuff, and organized everything, putting some stuff back in my car and the other stuff back where it belonged in the house.

I realized as I was sorting and cleaning up that this was a pretty accurate reflection of the clutter and chaos going on in the compartments and storage pockets of my mind and in my *life*.

Sometimes I just let all of the thoughts and emotions pile up. I stuff them into the glove compartment or center console of my mind and carry them around rather than throw them out or put them in their proper place. Then, when I am looking for something I really need, I have to go through all of that other unnecessary stuff to find it. It can be very frustrating and confusing. It can also be very exhausting to have to sort through thoughts and memories and resentments that should have been tossed out minutes or hours or days or weeks or months or years ago.

I have discovered that it is very important to my serenity to continually keep my vehicle and my mind in order as much as possible. I can do this by not just stuffing something away and by putting it where it actually belongs immediately. I can do this by not letting things pile up on top of each other. Sometimes stuff belongs in my vehicle and sometimes it doesn't. I have to make that choice.

When an emotion, resentment, or thought comes up in my mind, I have to make that same choice.

Does it belong in my mind?

Do I need to keep carrying it around, hidden and stuffed away? Is it in its proper place?

Just like my vehicle, I have to keep my mind in a neat, nonchaotic state.

It is much easier said than done for me. I really have to work at it, but it is possible.

Prayer, meditation, detachment, talking about it with a trusted person, writing the thought or what I am feeling down and seeing it on paper, giving it up to whatever higher power I believe in—these are some of the tools I can use to keep my mind clean. I am sure that there are many, many other tools that can be used for this purpose as well.

Suggestion: Try to not let the clutter build up in your vehicle and your mind.

Sort through your "stuff" in the moment whenever possible, and keep what you need and discard what you don't need. Picture yourself cleaning out your car and your mind at the same time. Hey, why not actually clean your car out once a week or once a month or whenever the clutter and chaos get to be too much, and while you're at it, clean that brain out too! Throw the clutter in the gutter! (Well, put it in a trash can, and then put the trash can out in the gutter to be emptied and taken to its proper place)

Drain the brain of pain and disdain!

FEAR-WHEEL DRIVE

Fear of driving.

I know many people who suffer from different self-imposed driving restrictions.

Some are afraid to drive on highways. Some are afraid to drive at night.

Some will only drive to certain places within certain boundaries. Some will not drive over a certain speed. Some won't drive in certain weather conditions. The list goes on and on.

I, myself, am afraid to drive a minivan lest I die of embarrassment. (I'm kidding, all of you minivan drivers, but feel free to run over this book a few times if I have offended you in any way!)

I've come to realize all of these driving fears can be applied to life.

Let's take a look at a couple of them. (C'mon with us all of you minivan drivers. By now I hope you've purchased another copy of the book to replace the one you ran over.)

Highway driving:

So many times in my life I have been afraid to join in with a big group of people because I felt like I did not fit in, or there were too many people who might not like me, or there were too many detrimental situations that could arise in a large group of people. Much like driving on a highway where there are all different types of people driving all different types of vehicles at varying degrees of speed and at all different levels of caution and safety.

I preferred to stay on my quiet little local roads where the chances of anything happening that I couldn't control seemed a lot less likely. Isn't this much like not making new connections with different people and just staying within my little group of friends and acquaintances? Or isolating myself when I feel like life has not gone the way I wanted it to? Fear of getting off of that little local road and not getting on the highway of life has often stopped me from going somewhere that may have been beautiful and exciting and new. It may have also saved me from getting into a ten-car pileup or getting lost in a strange place, but I believe that if I didn't ever get on the highway and take a risk of something bad happening, I would have missed out on some of the good things that happened.

Of course, one could make a case for staying on those little local roads and never venturing onto that crazy highway. If that works for you and you are content and happy with that, then by all means stay off of that on-ramp to the highway and keep to those local roads. Whatever works for you.

Driving within certain boundaries:

I have a friend who will only drive a certain distance north of their home and no further. I also have a friend who will not drive out of their home state.

It makes me think of my own life and how I have often been afraid to leave the supposedly safe boundaries I have set in my life, and even within myself.

How many times have I not expressed myself honestly because I was afraid to cross my own preset boundary? I'm not talking (no, I'm writing) about being offensive or insulting to someone. I'm talking (writing) about me not expressing my honest emotional state or feelings to another human being when doing so would be beneficial to my well-being, and possibly theirs as well. I'm talking (writing) about healthy communication that is so desperately needed for us to move forward as human beings on this planet.

I have set so many fearful boundaries based on low self-esteem and feelings of not being worthy enough that I have become afraid to drive across those self-imposed boundaries for fear of driving into the great unknown.

An unexpressed emotion for me can often turn into a resentment, and that can lead to a much more scary place than the great unknown. It can lead to the great known—that comfortable place where negativity and anger and depression are so familiar that I want to park right there and never put the car in drive again. If I stay in that space for too long, I might never get out of it, so I need to drive across those boundaries. I need to drive into another state (double entendre alert!). I need to broaden my scope of range, get out of myself, and move out into life.

So for me, all of the fear issues I have about driving can easily translate into fear issues I have about my life. That's really what this book is about. It all really boils down to lack of control and fear of the unknown. Fear of the unknown is what prevents us from moving forward and growing. Wanting to be in control of everything stops us from cooperating and empathizing with others.

I know for myself when I am driving on a well-maintained, well-lit highway or road, I always feel more safe and secure than driving on a dark road full of potholes and bumps.

Maintaining my spiritual fitness is much like maintaining a road. I have to make sure my internal landscape is always well lit and in good condition. The emotional potholes need to be filled with love. The route should have easy-to-read signs posted along the way in case I get lost. The signs that always lead me personally to a beautiful destination are patience, tolerance, and kindness. Generosity and empathy help too. Any sign that is created with love will always lead us away from Fear City. It is always a choice, and if I make the wrong choice in the moment, I can change direction at the next off-ramp.

Suggestion: Clichés are clichés for a reason, and here is a great one. The longest journey one will ever make is the journey from their head to their heart. I have nothing to add to that one.

VEHICLE I.D.

Do I define myself by the vehicle(s) I drive?

What do you drive?

Do you drive a compact hybrid or a gas-guzzling, four-wheel-drive pickup truck? Do you drive a practical four-door, four-cylinder sedan or a two-door, eight-cylinder muscle car?

Are you driving the kids around in a minivan or driving on the beach in a super-equipped SUV?

Are you driving a moderately priced vehicle or a vehicle that costs as much as some people's houses?

Whatever you are driving, are you judging someone else for what they are driving?

Do you think the hybrid driver is a tree-hugging hippie or the pickup driver is a Neanderthal jerk?

Do you think the four-door sedan driver is living a boring existence or the muscle car driver is an adrenaline-junkie show-off?

Do you think the person driving the minivan is unadventurous and dull or the person driving the ramped-up SUV is an extroverted egomaniac?

Do you think the person driving the moderately priced vehicle is average and middle class or the person driving the expensive vehicle is a wealthy, privileged boor?

Why are you judging, and where is it coming from?

At one point in my life, I was very successful and moderately wealthy. I had a very nice income, and I drove some very nice vehicles. I had eight vehicles in my name at one point, and each of them was brand new. SUVs, crossovers, sedans, and a muscle car all claimed a space in my driveway and garage. I felt good driving around in my brand-new vehicles and definitely had an air of superiority when I would see someone driving an older, less expensive vehicle than the one that I was in. Life was good!

Then, due to a perfect storm of financial catastrophes, some beyond and some within my control, the trajectory of my material world was disturbingly and violently altered. In a short period of time, the vehicles I so treasured were turned back in or sold, and I was left driving a fifteen-year-old pickup truck with 163,000 miles on it, while my spouse drove a five-year-old crossover with 90,000 miles on it. We did have two brand-new, bright, shiny bicycles though! Woo-hoo! Talk about a humbling experience. Though I must admit I saw it as more of a humiliating experience.

I felt inferior to anyone who was driving a newer, more expensive vehicle than the one I was forced to sit my angry butt in. I was comparing myself to all of the other vehicles, much as I had done when I was driving the new, shiny, luxury vehicles. Only now, I was comparing from the dark, inferior side of the highway of life rather than the well-lit and well-paved superior highway of life, and I didn't like it one bit.

It took many, many miles down a lot of dark and bumpy roads for me to finally see what I needed to do to get over my perceived misfortunes.

I had to realize that everyone driving their vehicles— whether new and expensive, or old and crappy, or old and expensive, or new and crappy—all had one thing in common.

Drumroll please. We were all *drivers*! We were all on the *same road*! It didn't matter what we were driving or what our final destinations were. At that moment in time, I was surrounded by drivers driving, and I was doing the exact same thing. I no longer had to compare my vehicle to theirs because it didn't matter anymore. We were all going from a point A to a point B. Some of us were equally angry. Some of us were equally calm. Some were more angry or less calm than others, but we were all *driving on the same road!* We all had something in common, even though we were all different. What a revelation! It opened my eyes and my mind and my *heart!*

I now see that I must always try to identify with the other drivers on the road rather than compare myself to them. When

I identify, I can see the similarities we all share as human beings. When I compare, I focus on the differences that as human beings we have a tendency to view negatively.

Why do we view differences negatively? Speaking for myself, because they scare the crap out of me! They usually cause me to come from a place of superiority or inferiority, and both of those places are located on Planet Fear. Now, because I can identify with another human's similarities to me, I can look past and actually appreciate and honor our differences as something necessary and beautiful. What a liberating experience not to have to judge and feel alienated because someone is different from me because I can see they are exactly the same as me at the same time.

If this doesn't make sense to you yet, please just act as if it does the next time you get behind the wheel of your vehicle. There is a saying in a certain fellowship that says, "Fake it till you make it." I'm asking you to try it until you are ready to buy it and see what road it leads you down. I believe when you see we are all part of the One, you will actually stop judging others and yourself. Let me make that a much more powerful "I" statement. I believe that when I see we are all part of the One, I will actually stop judging others and myself, and my outlook and attitude upon life will change for the better.

Suggestion: As I've just stated, try to see beyond the type of vehicle someone is driving and try to think of the similarities that they share with you. Then notice the differences of the vehicle they are driving and come from a place of nonjudgmental love when you do see the differences. I know this sounds corny and new age-y, but hey, you're reading this book for a reason, so just go with it for now! Over time, make these observations when you are *not* behind the wheel of a car. Do it while you are with your family, at work, or in line at the supermarket, and watch how your inner landscape shifts to a more calm and serene view.

You will be amazed at how everyone around you becomes less of a butthole when you change *your* thinking to identifying rather than comparing.

14

MISERY LOVES COMPANY

Rubbernecking.

What a word! It's very cartoonish but very accurate.

How often have I driven by the scene of a horrible collision and strained my neck to get a better look at the carnage and wreckage?

How often have I thanked God that it wasn't me in one of those vehicles, saying in hushed and wondrous tones something like, "Wow, if I had left my house five minutes sooner, that could have been me!"

Is it weird I'm actually selfishly grateful for someone else's misfortune? Is it horrible I kind of want to see just how bad the incident really is?

The same holds true when I see someone pulled over by those very pretty but ominous red and blue lights. I am always relieved it wasn't me (this time). I always wonder why they were pulled over. I can speculate and make up a whole story in the time it takes me to drive by them, based on ten seconds of observation. Oh, I'll bet they were texting on their phone!

Ha, that'll teach that Porsche to do 120 miles per hour in a 65-miles-per-hour zone!

I'll bet those guys got pulled over because they're *blank*. (Fill in your own very creative answer.)

Ask yourself if you have done the same. Give yourself an honest answer. Go deep for this one because it will reveal so much about yourself. I know I have been trying to find the source of my rubbernecking, and I believe that when I do (and I will), it will shed a light on so many other dark corners of my mind. I do know there is a difference between concern and curiosity. I do know it's different to discern than to judge, and I really have a gut feeling that rubbernecking ties into both ends of those energy dynamics. It is up to me which end I choose.

I have been on both sides of the situation. I have had my share of collisions, from multicar accidents, to hitting an inanimate object, and even to plowing down a deer that came out of nowhere, leaping across the road in a surreal split second.

I know the feeling of being gawked at as I stood next to what was once a pretty nice vehicle that became a total piece of scrap metal. Fingers pointed at me through rolled down windows. Looks of concerned relief that it wasn't them. Me babbling at the other drivers who were involved and trying to stay calm and speak coherently to the police on the scene.

Thank God I was never seriously injured. Thank God I never seriously injured anyone else except for one passenger who hit his head on the dashboard when I hit another vehicle before the days when seatbelts were mandatory.

The local and state police have pulled me over several times in a few different places (mostly for speeding and also for having very long hair back in the day).

I have felt the shame and embarrassment of sitting in my car while traffic slowed down to see why I had been pulled over—shaking heads, smirks, and sighs of relief that I was the one who got caught that day and not them. I could almost feel the judgement of others buzzing around me like a swarm of hungry mosquitoes as I sank lower and lower into my seat.

I hated the feeling of being held captive in my car, nervous and resentful, waiting for the cop to finish writing up the ticket(s) and to hand me my paperwork with a few stern words. The cop would say, "Be safe and have a good day!" as I slowly crawled off of the shoulder and cautiously made my way back into the flow of traffic, making sure to stay in the right lane and going exactly the speed limit.

Yeah, right. It's going to be a spectacular day now! The only things missing are a flat tire and a dead battery.

Rubbernecking. What is it that causes us as humans to slow down to the point of backing up traffic for miles just to view someone else's misery? Are we genuinely concerned, or are we genuinely curious and also a little morbidly excited by a tragedy that's not actually ours?

I've been in situations where rubbernecking has actually caused another collision between drivers who took their eyes off of the road to stare at other drivers who might have taken their eyes off of the road.

I've seen people take photos with their phones of bodies lying on the road. What a great social media post that'll make! How many likes will that one get?

I'm always a little shaken by man's inhumanity to man in those situations.

It has caused me many times to take a deep look inside.

Am I that selfish and self-centered that I would become a spectator to someone else's tragedy?

Have I become so numb and calloused that my compassion and empathy is overpowered by my desire to view another's bad luck? Is it that observing someone else's misfortunes takes the focus off of my own real or imagined misfortunes?

How do I explain it?

I think all of us humans have it in us somewhere. I believe it is a primal survival instinct that was probably used to teach us what not to do if we wanted to survive. Look at those hunters, Og and Oona, following those mastodons right over that cliff. We had better not do that! We want to live!

I am not a psychiatrist or a behavior expert, nor am I qualified to give any expert opinions on human nature or behavior other than my own experiences, but I do think the whole rubbernecking thing is one of the things about us humans that is not so attractive.

Suggestion: Next time you come across an incident on the road, try not to rubberneck.

If you do rubberneck, take a look at what it is bringing up for you right in that moment. Go deep with it. Try not to analyze it. Just look at it. Feel it. Before you know it, you will be past the scene, and maybe you will have learned a little more about who you really are.

CONTROLLING DISINTEREST

Most of the time when I get behind the wheel, I have a specific destination in mind.

I am driving to the store, to work, or to a friend's house. I am driving to a restaurant, to school, or to the beach. You get it.

Sometimes I just drive around to quiet my thoughts down or to get out of the house for an hour. (I wonder if that is a sort of destination?)

The point is, there is usually a beginning to my drive and an end. But what about the parts in between, you ask? (C'mon, I know those voices that I just heard are not in my own head!)

That's where things get really interesting, deep, confusing, and mysterious. The journey from point A to point B, and whatever other letters you might stop at along the way, is fraught (I have always wanted to use that word in a sentence! No, not *along!* Fraught!) with many unknowns.

When I get behind the wheel, I have no idea what will happen on the way to my destination.

Will there be traffic? Will I get into an incident? Will my car stall out? Will the driver in front of me slam on his brakes suddenly, causing my car to slam into his or hers? Will it rain? Will there be construction delays? The possibilities are endless, but the one thing that is certain is that some of them are seemingly within my control and others are completely out of my control. Some of the things I truly believe are in my control are, in reality, not.

For instance, I could say the speed I am driving is in my control, but is it really? Many different factors that influence my speed are actually out of my control.

The traffic conditions.

The weather conditions.

The drivers in front of me and behind me.

Etc., etc., etc.

But for argument's sake (that is such a strange expression), let's say there is no traffic, the weather is clear and calm, and there are no other drivers around me. I can then control the speed at which I am driving (provided of course that my vehicle has no issues).

I can control the volume of the music I am listening to. I can control the temperature of the heater and AC. Yet something could occur that could affect my control over these things as well.

So I guess what I am saying is that I really don't have much control over much of anything on the journey.

I can't control the traffic or the weather or the other drivers, and I have questionable control over many other seemingly controllable things—*much like life itself!*

Every day, I wake up, and I have some sort of destination in mind. I never know what is going to happen though at any given moment throughout my day. There are so many factors, so many mysteries, and so many unknowns.

An oil leak, a flat tire, a detour, a rain storm, and a traffic jam can all change my journey at any given moment just like an argument, a sneeze, a late train, good news, bad news, a salary increase, a salary decrease, the stock market, the line at the supermarket, and so on can all change my life's journey at any given moment. So what can I control, if anything?

I can control my responses to situations. I can control the words coming out of my mouth. I can control the way I treat others.

To be honest, there is really not much I can control. I used to believe I could control my emotions, but now I have come to realize I can't. The thing I can control is how I act out or respond to my emotions.

Let's say that anger comes up in a moment. There is no way in my opinion that I can control the anger because if I could, it would not come up in the first place. It's like saying I can control the rain once the rain has already started raining.

What I can control is what I do with that anger. Do I spew it all over everyone like boiling hot water spraying from a broken radiator hose, or do I feel it fully, go deep into it to see where it is really coming from, and then let it evaporate like the water escaping into the atmosphere from that broken radiator hose will eventually do?

If I fully face my anger, it will lose its power over me because I have owned it and not let it own me. By acknowledging it fully, I take away its power over me. I make the unknown known and therefore less fearful. I hope this makes sense to whomever is reading this because if you can grasp this extremely simple concept, I promise you your life will become more serene and joyous.

As I have grown older and presumably wiser, I have also realized how much I have missed out on by not noticing or paying attention to the things that occurred during my many journeys—all of the beautiful scenery and landscapes I ignored because I was so focused on getting somewhere ten minutes sooner. I missed many experiences both while driving and while living because I was so intent on getting somewhere rather than being somewhere. Now I try to not be concerned with getting somewhere or even being somewhere. I just try to focus on being. *Period.*

Suggestion: The next time you are driving somewhere, make note of how many unplanned situations occur during the drive. Feel whatever emotions come up for you, whether negative or positive, and embrace the emotion, fully allowing it to come to fruition. Then make a choice of how you will respond to it.

For example, another driver cuts you off and almost causes you to veer off the road. You get extremely angry and want to do something to the other driver. Feel the anger. Feel the resentment toward the other driver. Then decide how you will respond. If you decide to tailgate and then cut the other driver off, I wish you well on your journey to the hospital or to criminal court! If you decide not to take the other driver's action personally, which is very difficult to do at first, and then just simply forgive the other driver, I wish you well on your journey to peace of mind and serenity.

Do this same process of detachment and forgiveness even when you are not behind the wheel, and watch what happens. Also, allow yourself to fully enjoy your positive emotions that come up. Realize that a positive emotion is just as much out of your control as a negative one, and just embrace it as you would a negative emotion. If we learn what is driving our positive emotions, we can begin to manifest the energy that brings them up more and more and therefore experience them more frequently.

Win-win!

Also, try to relax into your journey. Let it unfold however it unfolds, and savor the moment-to-moment experiences that arise. You will eventually get to where you are going, whether it was where you were going or not.

16

PARKING SPOT ON

Parking.

Today I was sitting in my vehicle waiting for my spouse to come out of the store.

It's a huge parking lot, and there are quite a few stores, so it's always pretty full.

As I sat there, I observed a car coming down the aisle from one direction, and another car coming down the same aisle from the opposite direction. There was one open space, and it became apparent they were both going for it.

One driver put her signal light on, indicating that she was going to pull in, and the other driver sped up as soon as he saw her signal and proceeded to pull into the space a split second before the other car could. *Oh boy*, I thought to myself. *This is not going to be pretty.* I was getting ready to witness a nasty confrontation but instead I saw something that gave me hope for mankind.

The woman who had been so rudely cut off simply smiled and waved at the man who had selfishly taken the space and continued on to the next aisle. I was pleasantly shocked.

I saw her pull into an open space and I thought to myself, *Here it comes. She's going to key that guy's car as she walks by it, or at the very least put a nasty note under his wiper. Maybe even let the air out of one of his tires!*

She didn't do any of those things. She just continued casually walking into the store. She had a look on her face like she was listening to some kind of calm, inner dialogue.

I was amazed and confused.

I know I probably would have had a fit if that had been me. I wouldn't have done any damage to the other guy's car, but I definitely would have ranted and raved like a lunatic to myself. I would have gone through quite a few ugly scenarios of what I would have liked to happen to that thoughtless jerk. I would have carried that anger and resentment for the rest of the day and then suffered an emotional hangover filled with guilt and shame over my thoughts.

That kind and gentle woman showed me what dignity and grace looks like. She was an example of how forgiveness is the way to peace of mind and serenity. With one simple act, she demonstrated what true forgiveness looks like.

I've heard it said that when the only tool I have in my toolbox is a hammer, every situation looks like a nail. I'm so grateful I have many tools in my toolbox, and I'm grateful to have been so gently and powerfully reminded of that by what I witnessed today in the parking lot.

Suggestion: The next time you are jockeying like a crazy person for that one space in that crowded parking lot, call off the race and let the other driver have it.

You may have to wait a little longer or walk a little farther, but I guarantee you will experience serenity and peace of mind by being so unselfish. That's worth more than a six-by-twelve-foot piece of asphalt any time.

CHANGING LANES IN VAIN

I drive on one of New York's busiest and most congested highways. The Long Island Expressway, or LIE for short (there's a big dose of irony for you), is known as the world's biggest parking lot. During peak travel times, it is 71.02 miles of frustrating, mind-numbing traffic jams. The funny thing is that traffic will be at a dead stop one minute and then all of a sudden will speed up to sixty-five miles per hour for a minute and then come to a sudden dead stop again. It's soul crushing. It really is a challenge for me not to feel like every single driver in every single vehicle woke up that morning and thought of ways to screw me on the road. If I had passengers, they would definitely be named Vic and Tim.

Vic and Tim and I would talk about how bad the other drivers were and how they were all out to get us, especially me because I'm the driver.

We would notice how every time that I changed from a slow-moving lane to a faster-moving one, the faster one would instantly come to a dead stop, and the lane I had just vacated was now the faster one.

They would point out how the universe was once again sticking it right up old Richie's butt.

They would call my attention to the fact that all of the other drivers were indeed conspiring against me, making sure to keep me boxed in and trapped no matter what lane I chose to be in.

They would speculate that the other drivers were somehow all in direct communication with each other and executing a very well thought-out plan against poor me. The worse that traffic became, the more frustrated I would become and the more convinced I was that Vic and Tim were indeed very insightful and completely right about everything.

I can't tell you how many times this scenario has played out in my head.

I've actually screamed out a tirade of F-bombs and other choice anatomical descriptions while pounding on the steering wheel and gritting my teeth in pure rage at all of the dirty dog conspirators who were very successfully thwarting my attempt to arrive at my destination in a timely manner. Talk about paranoia. Talk about self-pity. Talk about victimization. It's amazing I could crawl down that rabbit hole all because I couldn't seem to choose the right lane to be in at any given moment.

I often wonder how I could let something as meaningless as a lane change sway me to such extreme thinking and fill me with so much rage and self-loathing—pretty heavy stuff, and something I am definitely not proud of.

How could I project so much fear and frustration out onto and into every single vehicle that shared that very same traffic-clogged road with me?

Why would I think they were all out to get me and not anyone else?

Here's why. (I think.)

We are raised to believe we need to get ahead—that we need to be quicker, more decisive, have more of an idea where we are going than everyone else. It's what gives us an advantage and therefore more power than the next person.

I will speak for myself now.

I have transferred that belief system into every aspect of my life. Especially driving. Yes. Driving.

That cocoon I call a vehicle has become a space where I am separate from all of the other drivers, and I enforce that belief by trying to get ahead of them all while not letting any of them get ahead of me.

I do it very angrily. I feel cheated by the universe when it doesn't go my way, and I feel hatred for all of the other drivers. Wow. (Please do not be afraid of me, as the hatred fades once I come to my senses.)

When I look at it from outside of myself, I see how vain and ridiculous it actually is.

Every other driver on the road at the same time as me is in exactly the same traffic I am in.

Are some of them thinking about me what I'm thinking about them? That would be horrible because I'm not out to get anyone. I'm just trying to get to where I am going as quickly and painlessly as possible.

Ohhhhh. So maybe the same holds true for them as well.

Maybe (as unbelievable as it may seem) they are not even thinking about me!

Maybe they have their own thoughts and trials and tribulations.

Maybe some of them couldn't give a rat's ass about the traffic and are cool, calm, and collected about it all.

Who knows? I certainly don't.

I can tell you what I do know.

When I let it go, when I don't take it personally, when I stop listening to Vic and Tim and throw them out of the car, guess what happens?

C'mon, take a guess.

If you guessed that I find peace and serenity, you guessed correctly.

If you guessed that I stop hating the other drivers and making them my victimizers and start seeing them as just some other human beings going through some of the same things I am going through, you guessed correctly.

If you guessed that I starting ramming other vehicles with mine and got some satisfaction out of it before being arrested, then you need to go back and reread the previous chapters, you sick little puppy.

Suggestion: When you are feeling like all of the other drivers are against you, take a pause and ask yourself if you really are all that important. Ask yourself why you would think they are even aware of you specifically. Ask yourself if you feel that way about one of them, that you are out to get one of them specifically.

You will see things differently. I promise.

A friend once told me this: "The world conspiracy against me has been called off due to a lack of interest."

Believe that is true, and you will find peace and serenity.

You'll get to where you are going even if it takes a little longer, and you will feel much better than if you got there two minutes sooner and ten times angrier.

18

BACK IN THE U.S.S. CAR

Back seat driving.

I call shotgun! I don't know many people who like to be relegated to the back seat. It seems to carry a built-in negative connotation. Back. Step back. Back away. Taking a step backward. You can't go back.

I'm sure you clever devils can think of a few more. Just scribble them right there in the margins. I won't be offended or taken *aback*.

Not only do I not like being dumped into the back seat, I also don't like being called a back seat driver when I am.

The committee in my head immediately calls an emergency meeting to discuss this precarious predicament. Some of them will be saying, "Do you know who I am?" or, "I have millions of miles and years of driving experience. How dare they stick me back here? What will people think?" The committee in my head is always voting unanimously for all of my thoughts and ideas, by the way. No matter how ridiculous an idea of mine may seem, it always gets a resounding *yes* vote from every member.

Would you like to know why?

It's because I appointed all of them to the committee, so of course they are going to go my way! Isn't that great? I'll bet lots of you have your own head committee too!

I'd also bet they have steered you over a cliff or into a ditch many, many times. I know that mine has.

Anyway, back to being a back seat driver and why I don't like sitting in the lowly back seat.

I think it definitely has everything to do with me not being in control. I have no control over the vehicle. I mean, there are no pedals or steering wheel in the back seat. No speedometer. No gauges. No windshield. Just empty space between me and the driver and the very important person in the front passenger seat. I can't even fiddle with the music or temperature controls.

I can't unlock the childproof locks or unlock or lock the power windows.

Quite frankly, it sucks.

All I can do is sway nauseatingly back and forth while my spine is dislocated by every bump in the barely visible (from the back seat) road.

Being in the back seat is practically one step away from being towed behind the vehicle on a sheet of plywood. Can you tell I don't like sitting in the back seat?

This is why I may occasionally feel the need when I am sitting grudgingly (no, really?) in the back to offer my wisdom to the driver.

I need to feel like a part of the action. I need to be needed. What better way to do that than by sharing my experience behind the wheel with whomever is driving—whether they have asked me to or not. So what if I'm distracting them or making them nervous? Hey, you just missed the exit! Are you even listening to me?

Don't they know who I am?

I have millions of miles and years of driving experience!

It seems to be the same with me giving advice even when there is no vehicle wrapped around us.

Don't they know who I am?

I have millions of life experiences I can share with them—whether they have asked me to or not!

My opinion is very valuable! To me at least. I can't tell you how many times I have given my unsolicited advice or opinion and it has not turned out well. It reminds me of an instance with Tzoneh, an Apache elder of mine. I had offered someone who we were both talking to some unsolicited advice on a situation they were in, and they got very defensive and offended.

After they had walked away, Tzoneh turned to me, and in a very quiet voice said, "Rich, would you like my opinion on what just happened?"

I said, "Sure!"

He said in an even quieter voice, "I try to never miss an opportunity to mind my own business."

You could have knocked me over with a feather.

Ever since then, I really do try not to give driving directions or instructions unless I am asked.

The same goes for opinions or advice.

Here is what I have learned.

If my intention when I am giving directions, advice, or opinions is to be in control of the situation, then it usually will not end well. That's because I have an ulterior motive.

However, if I am truly trying to be helpful with an unselfish intention, and if I am asked, then I am more than happy to share my driving or life experiences with whomever asks for it. Very simple and very effective.

Suggestion: The next time you are in the back seat, try to refrain from giving your unsolicited directions. The same goes for when you are in a conversation and no one is asking for your opinion or advice.

If someone does ask, pause for a moment to check what your intention is with the advice or opinion you are about to inject into their life. Is it self-serving, or is it to be genuinely helpful?

Remember you can't get the bullet back once you pull the trigger. The same is true with our advice and opinions. They don't have a reverse gear.

Drive and speak safely, my friends.

You are not alone on the highway of life.

THE INVISIBLE MAN

Have you ever stopped at a red light on a deserted street in the wee hours of the morning, no other vehicles in sight? It's just you and the red light. Have you ever been on a stretch of straight, open highway with no other vehicles around for miles?

Did you wait until the light turned green to go? Did you obey the speed limit on the deserted highway?

If you answered yes, do you know why you did?

I think I know what the reason is for me, and it's pretty simple.

They are laws. True, they are man-made laws, but they are still laws. They are things I've been taught and have obeyed ever since I started driving. (And no, my first car wasn't a Flintstones-type car. It actually had rubber tires and wasn't made of wood and stone.)

I think I have been made aware of the consequences for running a red light or speeding, and I don't want to experience them, so

I sit there at the red light, patiently or sometimes impatiently waiting for it to turn green. I don't go over the speed limit even though I am tempted to just floor it and feel that thrill of speed for a few moments.

So even though I probably could break these laws and never suffer any consequences (besides maybe a little twinge of guilty conscience), I don't.

What we have here is an example of the biggest law in the universe. (No, not the law that says if you want to become rich and famous, then do something really vain, obnoxious, vile, or despicable, and make sure to upload it to every possible social media page so it's imprinted onto mankind's consciousness for all of eternity.)

It's the law of (insert cosmic drumroll here) cause and effect.

If I go through that red light or go faster than the speed limit, I put into motion actions that will have an effect.

Some possible effects include the following:

- a cop who I didn't notice hiding somewhere pulling me over for running the light or speeding
- a car I didn't see for some reason entering the intersection and colliding with me
- a vehicle seemingly out of nowhere stopped in the road and me ramming into it
- a pedestrian crossing the road and me hitting them
- an animal running onto the highway and me not being able to stop in time
- a red-light camera that will send an expensive ticket in the mail

You get the drift.

The effects might not always be immediate or violent. They might never be known to us. That doesn't mean they aren't there.

Some effects can take time to appear, and they can be learning experiences, but there will always be an effect after a cause. Remember: universal law.

You might say, "Ha! I have driven through red lights and nothing has ever happened to me! No ticket, no collision, no hitting a pedestrian, and no guilty conscience. I have gone over the speed limit more times than I can count and never received a ticket. Zip, zero, zilch! So there go your laws right out the window!"

To which I say this: We, as humans on this plane, do not always get to see what's going on behind the curtain. Most of the time we are unaware of all of the ripples our actions cause when cast upon the waters of humanity. Here is where the human version of cause and effect differs from the universal version. The human version contains emotion, perception, attachment, and judgement. The universal version does not.

The human version is open to our human interpretation of effects.

The universal version, being of spirit, is not.

The universal law of cause and effect is pure and eternally consistent. It never wavers. It gives us exactly what we ask for. Always.

Our thoughts, our actions, and our intentions are the cause, and the universe responds with the effects of what we think. Simple, pure, unwavering—just like the red light. Just like the speed limit sign.

The red light is there. The speed limit sign is there. They don't have any attachments or judgements on whether we obey them or not. We make that choice, and in choosing we create a cause that then has an effect. We can't blame the red light for whatever happens once we go through it. We can't blame the speed limit sign if we go faster than mandated.

We can't blame the universe for whatever happens once we think or intend something. The universe is giving us exactly what we are asking for with our thoughts, actions, and intentions. It cannot do anything but that. We are the cause of our effects. We set the wheels in motion, and if they happen to run over us, it is because of our thoughts, actions, and intentions.

The universe does not judge our thoughts, actions, or intentions. It only responds to them. It is not vindictive, vengeful, or spiteful. It is the opposite of all of those things. So try to remember that when you are thinking or acting a certain way. Try to see what your true intention is. You will get what you give out.

One more thing. The universe will keep giving you the opportunity to learn what you need to learn, no matter how many times it takes. If your intention is to not be an angry person anymore, it will send you many opportunities to practice not being angry. If your intention is to not be impatient anymore, it will keep sending you opportunities to learn patience, and so on and so forth with any intention you set.

Suggestion: The next time you are waiting at a red light that you could go through or driving the speed limit that you could easily surpass, imagine what some of the effects might be. Try to think of the obvious ones and also the not-so-obvious ones.

Try to do the same thing when you are thinking about something.

Picture the effects of whatever it is you are thinking about, and then decide whether or not you want to keep thinking what you are thinking or change what you are thinking.

Watch what happens.

20

THE I OF THE STORM

This week, we had the remnants of a hurricane pass through our area.

It brought huge, record downpours and fierce winds with it, and many major highways and several side roads were closed for a period of time.

Of course, this happened the day before my spouse, Cyn, and I were supposed to travel the hundred plus miles to our storage unit to finally start emptying it out.

We decided to go ahead with our plan, and we left the following morning, full of determination.

We programmed our GPS to use as a backup because we didn't know if our usual routes were closed.

It turned out that most of them were closed, and it took us five and a half hours for a drive that would have normally taken us two hours.

At one point, it took us an hour to go two miles. We were boxed into our lane by tractor trailers on all sides, so we couldn't even see what was going on up ahead, to our rear, and to our sides. It was very, very frustrating. The GPS was constantly chiming in with that annoying "updating route" message.

There were frequent road closures and detours. Some of the detours had three or four lanes of already nightmarish traffic suddenly squeezing down into one lane to exit the road. No one would give an inch to let the other vehicles into their lane, so the process was exceedingly slow and heavy. The air was charged with anger and frustration. I am sure you can imagine all of the joy and serenity all of the drivers were experiencing in those precious moments. (Sarcasm alert!)

Through it all, I am very happy to report my spouse and I stayed relatively calm, and even though there were many twists and turns thrown into our journey, we dealt with them using all of the tools in our toolboxes.

Patience. Humor. Acceptance. Tolerance. Faith. Positivity. Music. Spiritual conversations. Light conversations.

We dropped all of our expectations and just went with the flow—sometimes literally, as the roads were actually flooded, and water was flowing across them.

Each time one of us was ready to blow a gasket, the other would crack a joke, talk about a positive subject, or put on a song we both loved, and we were able to keep the atmosphere light and stress- free.

Much like life, we really didn't have much control over the circumstances that had caused so many delays and changes to our journey. All we could control was our responses to the ever-changing landscapes. We made choices and then dealt with the effects as they unfolded.

No anger or impatience. No being victims. No resentments.

We just stayed focused in the moment and made our way forward.

Eventually, we arrived at our destination, a little tired and stiff, but content with the fact that we hadn't let any negativity creep in and flavor our experience. We were happy that the GPS had not been smashed or thrown out the window. (It had definitely tempted us a few times, but cooler heads prevailed.)

We were amazed at how well we had cooperated with each other and with the universe. Here we had two people who had a history of being aggressive, angry drivers, and yet neither one of us was being led away in handcuffs, even though there had been plenty of opportunities to practice extreme violence and destruction.

I can only speak for myself, but I have to say it was because I had made conscious choices not to react fearfully. I had made conscious choices to react lovingly. (No, I wasn't running around hugging the other drivers!)

Fear drives anger, frustration, impatience, revenge, and being uncooperative, whereas love drives tolerance, patience, acceptance, and forgiveness.

That's the road I want to drive on. It makes the journey that much more palatable.

Suggestion: Find an area where a hurricane or major storm (either literally or figuratively) has just been through, and decide if and how you want to travel through it. Remember that the way you choose to travel through it will affect your experiences on the journey.

Note: Hopefully you got the symbolism of the hurricane or major storm being situations and circumstances in your life. (I know, I know! You're not stupid! Sorry!)

21

OH! KLA HOME A

For the past twenty or more years, my family and I have traveled to Oklahoma.

We have been adopted into several families within the Cheyenne-Arapaho tribe, and that has provided us with a reason to visit frequently over the years. My adopted Cheyenne dad (may he rest in peace) always got a huge laugh out of the way we New Yorkers drive.

He would wonder where we were always going in such a rush. I could see the look of amusement in his eyes when we would "stop" at a stop sign. He'd always say, "Man, I guess you guys from New York spell *slow* differently than we do in Oklahoma. We spell it *s-l-o-w,* but you guys spell it *s-t-o-p!*"

He pointed out that anyone he's ever driven with in or from New York just kind of rolls on through stop signs without ever really stopping.

He also noticed that a yellow light means speed up to us New Yorkers, whereas in Oklahoma it means slow down because the light is about to turn red.

One time when he was visiting us in New York, we were driving up the thruway to visit some friends, and there was a pretty big traffic jam.

I could feel him observing me as I got more and more angry and frustrated with the vehicles around me. I knew that he could sense my inner boiling rage even though on the outside I was trying to put on a calm front. At one point he asked me, "Hey Rich, do you think that those guys will still be there when we get there, or do you think they will sell their house and move?"

I looked at him with a very puzzled expression. "Dad, how the heck would they have sold their house and moved in the hour that it's taking us to get there?"

"I don't know Rich, but you're sure acting like they could."

I instantly got his point, and the whole atmosphere in the car changed because the whole atmosphere inside me changed.

Trust me when I tell you that driving in Oklahoma is a much more laid-back experience than driving in New York. The speed limit on most of their roads is sixty-five or seventy miles per hour, and that seems to be good enough for most people. I, however, see it a little differently. That's because my brain is trained to add a ten- to fifteen-mile-per-hour extension onto the speed limit.

Sometimes I wish someone would write a book explaining how the way I think about driving reflects the way I think about life. Hopefully one day somebody will. (Wink wink.)

Anyway, I've noticed I definitely drive less aggressively when I am in Oklahoma, but it's still more aggressive than most Oklahomans.

I also have a tendency to be more courteous and less combative, allowing people to merge in front of me and to pull out in front of me without cursing or gesturing like a lunatic.

I've learned that being around considerate drivers actually rubs off and causes me to become more considerate. What a concept! Like-minded drivers attract like-minded drivers!

Angry drivers attract other angry drivers. Inconsiderate drivers attract other inconsiderate drivers. Aggressive drivers attract other aggressive drivers.

Does that mean patient drivers attract other patient drivers?

Cautious drivers attract other cautious drivers?

Courteous drivers attract other courteous drivers?

I would love to answer those questions with a resounding *yes*, but unfortunately that has not been entirely true in my experience.

Here's why I think that is so.

I am not completely willing to believe it.

I am not completely ready to participate in that dynamic.

I say I am, but I do not actually do it.

I am still attached to my old, comfortably painful way of thinking instead of a new, uncomfortably pain-free way of thinking.

So if I am thinking this way, then how can I expect other drivers not to? Why should they change their way of thinking if I am not willing to?

It all comes down to this.

I have to take personal responsibility for myself. I have to change *my* thinking because I certainly can't change yours. I have to do it willingly without any attachment to the outcome.

I have to change even if no one else is willing to change because I can only control the vehicle I am driving. I can't control the one I am not. And here's a totally crazy statement: the only way I can be free is to completely and utterly surrender.

By surrendering my thinking to the power of cosmic law, I set myself free, and that is when other like-minded, freely-surrendering people start appearing in my life, and I start appearing in theirs.

Crazy, right? But entirely true.

Just think about it.

In a traffic jam where everyone is trying to merge down to one lane, if every person let one person into their lane, the traffic would flow like a river rather than a jumbled-up, chaotic mess. The drivers who were extended a courtesy by other drivers would extend that same courtesy to other drivers, and so on. That's how life is supposed to work. That's how traffic flows rather than meanders.

So simple. So pure. So natural.

Suggestion: Try to think of others when driving.

Believe me, I know it's not easy.

Try to let someone in when merging.

Slow down and let someone into your path. Think of it as not having another driver doing something *to* you, but rather you doing something *for* another driver.

You will see a difference. I promise, but more importantly, cosmic law guarantees it.

IT'S NOT PERSONAL; IT'S PERSONAL

I would guess that my vehicle starts 999 times out of 1,000. The odds might even be better than that.

I never even give it any thought—until that one time it doesn't start.

Then it becomes the only thing I can think about.

I'd love to say I take it with a grain of salt (What the hell does that expression mean? Who puts one grain of salt on anything?), but usually I go right into victim mode.

Why is this crap happening to me?

This car is a piece of garbage! The dealership I bought it from screwed me!

The universe is telling another joke, and once again I'm the punch line.

On and on and on.

What I usually fail to realize in the moment is that there are a variety of reasons why it won't start. Some of them are obvious, like a dead battery or no fuel in the tank, but there can also be many other reasons that are not so obvious.

Some of the reasons require me to take personal responsibility while other causes may simply be beyond my control, like a loose wire or a computer glitch. (Is there anything left in this world that doesn't have a computer in it?) At some point in my thought process, I have to pause and talk myself down off of the ledge so I can calmly and rationally move on to the solution.

First let's look at a couple of the things that are obviously my responsibility.

No fuel in the tank: I love to test that letter *E* on the fuel gauge. Guess what? It doesn't stand for endless or estimated. It means *empty*!

That one is definitely my personal responsibility for driving by the gas station ten times and finding eleven excuses for not stopping.

Dead battery: If I left an interior light on or my headlights on or a device plugged in for an inordinate amount of time, then that's on me.

If I didn't take the time to check every once in a while to see if there was so much corrosion on the battery terminals that they looked like two mounds of snow, then that's on me. If I've had the same battery in the vehicle for five years, then that's on me. You get it.

Some of the less obvious causes may also be because I did not take the vehicle in for scheduled maintenance or I ignored a warning light, so I could take some responsibility for those.

A computer glitch or a worn or malfunctioning part that is buried in the engine or a clog in the fuel system would be beyond my control but again may have been diagnosed with proper maintenance. So even these could be partially on me.

See my point? I always have to look at my part in a situation, however small it may be.

Sometimes my part may be just to accept that there are things beyond my control. Now there's a huge word. Accept.

Once I accept something, then I can begin to move forward. I can look for a solution to a problem once I accept that there is a problem. Being afraid of a problem and burying my head in the sand does not solve a problem. Being afraid of a problem and looking at it despite my fear of it is the beginning of a solution to the problem.

Once I face it head on, it immediately starts to lose its grip on me, and I can begin to move through it to a solution.

Sometimes the solution may not be exactly what I want it to be, or it may be painful or difficult, but it will appear.

Just like a huge car repair bill, it may be hard to swallow, but the end result will be the car running again.

Sometimes it might not be a huge repair bill. It could be just a simple fix. Whatever it is, it will work out however it is supposed to, and the key is my acceptance of the solution.

Suggestion: Try to remember that keeping up with vehicle maintenance is essential if you want a reliably starting vehicle. Control what you can control, and accept what you can't control.

Apply the same principles to your emotional and spiritual maintenance, and your spirit will reliably start when you turn the key!

23

GIVE ME A SIGN

Road signs. Where would we be (literally) without them?

So many signs. So many instructions. So many rules. So many guidelines. Let's take a cruise on down the road and take a look at some of them.

<u>Yield right of way:</u> When I was a kid, I used to think someone made a grammatical mistake on this one. I thought, *Shouldn't it say "yield right away"?* I didn't see that it was actually correct and telling approaching drivers to give the vehicles that were supposed to proceed before them the "right of way."

How many times in my life did I blow right through this one? I wasn't going to yield my right of way to anyone! Not my parents, not my teachers, not my friends, not my spouse, not my kids. The list goes on and on. By not yielding, I certainly created my share of collisions, near misses, and close calls. But I showed them, whoever them was!

Instead of letting traffic flow rhythmically and naturally, I decided my right of way was the right way. Screw all the other drivers.

Unlike the Tao, which tells us that by bending like a tree in the strong wind we will never break, I chose to stand rigid and fight the wind. Do I need to tell you how that always ended up? Bent fenders. Dented bumpers. Broken headlights. Shattered taillights. Arguments. Hurt feelings. Self-indulgence. Rationalization and justification galore!

When I yield right of way, all sorts of things happen. The traffic flows as it should. I cooperate with the other drivers. My blood pressure goes down. I feel better about myself. I surrender to the ebb and flow of the traffic. I can do that in life as well.

Surrender to the ebb and flow of the universe, allowing life to wash over me rather than fighting the current and eventually giving up and being swept away.

Slow down: This one is pretty self-explanatory. It tells me I am approaching an area that needs to be navigated at a speed slower than the speed I am currently driving. How many times in life do I need to proceed at a speed that is slower than the speed I am living at, or thinking at, or reacting at? Am I making a hasty decision based on anger, greed, or lust? Am I reacting quickly to a person or a situation out of envy, defensiveness, or judgement?

When I *slow down,* it gives me the opportunity to take in the scenery or observe the traffic conditions around me. Slowing down allows me to become more aware. I become more conscious of the turns and the road conditions. I make clearer decisions and react calmly. I navigate the road with a greater awareness than if I was just barreling through haphazardly.

Wait a minute! What if I do that in my everyday life? What if I apply *slow down* to my thoughts and emotions? Could it be? Would I actually become a calmer, more relaxed human? If you are thinking yes, then you are right! Give yourself a cookie (or whatever other nonharmful thing you do to reward yourself)! Now, go out and try it on the road and in your life. You will be amazed. I guarantee it.

Curves ahead: Short and sweet. It's telling me there are curves ahead. That means I need to adjust my speed and really pay attention to the road ahead.

I don't know about you, but my life is definitely curvy. It's certainly not a straight, easily navigable road.

It twists and turns in all different directions, and it would be great to have a heads up whenever life has *curves ahead.*

Here's some good news! We as humans have a built-in *curves ahead* sign. It's called intuition.

It's that feeling you get in your solar plexus or your chest or whatever chakra is lighting up at the moment. It's a warning sign that you are about to enter conditions that require you to use your brakes and steering wheel to navigate through those curves ahead. (By now, I'm sure you clever devils are aware that your brakes and steering wheel are your emotional awareness.)

If you heed the *curves ahead* sign, the curves ahead certainly won't disappear. You will just be aware that you are approaching them and be able to navigate them with more awareness, just like life.

Stop: This is a great one. In a previous chapter, I mentioned my adopted Cheyenne dad had always commented about how New Yorkers must spell the word *slow* as *s-t-o-p* because we just kind of roll through stop signs rather than come to a full stop. (This is true in my case. I cannot speak for all New Yorkers, but you know who you are!)

In my experience, I can tell you I have rolled through the stop sign between my brain and my mouth many, many times when I wish I hadn't. Had I made a full stop and looked both ways before I said or wrote something that would have been better off unsaid or unwritten, I would not have felt the effects of the collision and chaos that running that mental stop sign caused.

Much like driving my vehicle through a stop sign on the road, I can cause a lot of harm by going through the stop sign in my head.

Four-way stop: Would you like to do a quick study on human behavior? Sit at a four-way stop for an hour and observe what goes on.

Watch as some people ignore the rule. Watch as some people follow the rule. What is the rule?

When two vehicles arrive at a four-way stop at the same time side-by-side, *the vehicle to the right has the right of way*. If three vehicles arrive at the same time, the car farthest left should continue to yield until both of the other cars to the right of them have passed. Easy peasy—if you're a physicist!

Here's another one: *The first car to pull up to the stop sign is the first car that gets to proceed.* If cars are all stopping at the intersection at different times, each should proceed through in the order they arrived. It doesn't matter what direction a car is going either.

Much easier to understand.

And one more: *Four-way stops always operate in a clockwise direction.* So the car farthest to the right always has the right of way, and then cars take their turns in a clockwise direction. If multiple cars approach a four-way stop at about the same time, the driver who comes to a complete stop first proceeds first. Yikes and double yikes!

This is all very confusing to me. Different interpretations of the same situation, just like in life! Who would have thought?

I've watched people be considerate and wave other drivers on, and I've watched people be inconsiderate and just go regardless of their position in the intersection. I've seen collisions and near misses. I've seen fights break out. I've also seen courtesy and consideration when someone waves another driver through even if they had the right of way. (Remember that one?).

Many times in my life, I have waved others through. Just as many times, I have jumped my place in the intersection. Courtesy has always felt better than impatience. I don't always practice it, which I find odd because I'd much rather feel good. I used to say to myself when I was selfish or impatient, *Well, I'm just not there yet,* but that seems a little self-serving to me now. If I tell myself I'm not there yet, then it stands to reason that's what my spiritual condition will look like and therefore my life.

However, if I act with courtesy and consideration, then my life will look and feel better because I am aligning my outside with my inside. (My partner loves saying that and actually living it.)

It's all so complicated and yet so simple, much like the rules of the four-way stop.

Caution work zone: You're driving along, and you see this sign. You can be on a highway, a city street, or a country road, and it means the same thing on any of them. The road conditions are about to change. There may be work crews on the road and on the sides of the road. There may be a flagger. The pavement might be torn up or very bumpy. There may be big trucks with flashing lights.

Traffic will slow down or stop altogether. Then all of a sudden, you are past the work zone, the road improves, and the traffic starts flowing normally again. All is right in your vehicular world. Later on, if and when you pass that section of road and the work is done on it, it's like the crews, equipment, and rough road conditions were never even there.

Wow! Isn't life just like that?

We are cruising along. Things are going smoothly—no bumps and no traffic. Then boom, all of a sudden we are in a situation or a problem arises. We have to set up a "work zone" to deal with it. We may call in our higher power. We may need our guardian angels, spiritual guides, teachers, and our heavy equipment brought in. (You can use whatever metaphors or symbols work for you in this section. You may not believe in any sort of higher power, guides, teachers, or angels. That's fine! Your crew can consist of whatever crew members work for you. After all, it's your road.)

So now we get to work. We tear things up. We smooth out the bumps. We may have to reroute some things. We may have some unexpected delays. Things may slow down. There may be some irritation. There may be pain. We may want things to move faster or in a different direction.

All of these things are much like the work zone we are in when we are driving. Just like when we are behind the wheel and not able to control the work zone conditions on the road, sometimes we cannot control the work zone conditions of our lives.

We have to let the crew do the work they know how to do. We have to remember that once we get through the work zone, the road will once again be smooth—until we come to the next work zone.

Suggestion: When you are caught in a work zone, try to take in all of the hard work that's being done on your behalf to make the road easier to navigate (but make sure not to take your eyes off what is going on ahead of you!). Tell yourself this is only a temporary situation and that the road will soon be clear and smooth. Just like your life.

24

LIFE CAN BE FOGGED UP

Fog. I like this word. Fog. Pretty much sounds like what it is.

Driving in fog can be extremely difficult and nerve-wracking.

The fog causes us really to focus on what is directly in front of us because we can't actually see too far ahead. It draws our attention to the immediate area of road ahead. That can sometimes be a few feet (or meters if you're metric). The fog doesn't allow us to see down the road. We can't see too far to either side or to our rear. We are pretty much enveloped in an envelope (our vehicle) within an envelope (the fog). (Am I using too many parentheses in this chapter?) (I hope not!)

Sometimes I find myself in a spiritual, mental, or emotional fog. I feel very much alone and insecure. I feel engulfed and shrouded by something I can't even hold on to. (Next time you're in fog, try grabbing a handful and putting it in a container!)

This type of fog can be caused by worry, resentment, envy, greed, or any of the fear-based emotions. It can cause me to go into a very deep state of anxiety or panic. It can certainly keep me guessing about what lies ahead down the road that is blocked from my view.

Not knowing what is coming up ahead can be extremely frightening, behind the wheel and in life.

When I was younger and less experienced, I would turn on my high beams to try to see through the fog, but that only made it worse because the light would reflect off of the fog and back into my eyes. (I am so old that when I first started driving, fog lights were not readily available as an option.) This made it even more difficult to navigate through the fog. I finally learned I had to just drive slowly and cautiously, hoping to catch a glimpse of the taillights of the vehicle ahead of me. I had to trust that the drivers ahead of me and behind me were doing the same thing. I had to stay keenly aware of whatever obstacles might suddenly appear at the last minute through the fog and hopefully react in time. It was not a fun experience. Sometimes I would catch a glimpse of a streetlight or an illuminated store sign, and that would ease my anxiety a little. Sometimes, depending on the time of morning, the sun would rise and burn the fog away. Sometimes I would just pull over and wait for the fog to lift.

In my life, I have learned that much like driving in the fog, if I turn my high beams on when I am navigating through a spiritual, mental, or emotional fog, the light will reflect back at me. Reflection of this type of fog can also be difficult to navigate through because I may not want to see what is being reflected back. I have to remember it might be better for me to take it slowly and cautiously. I have to remember that sometimes I have to use just my low beams so the fog reflects back less. Sometimes a light may be visible from another source, and it may shine a different yet helpful light. I may not even know exactly where that light is coming from. I have to have faith that I have the ability to navigate through the fog if I use my experience and skills in a calm manner.

I also have to tell myself that the fog is temporary, and it will eventually lift. The situations in life are also temporary and will eventually lift. When I get out of the fog, I have a little bit more skill than I did before I drove through it. I am a little bit more experienced than I was before. When I get through a situation in life, I have a little more skill at dealing with life, and I have added to my life experiences.

Suggestion: When driving through fog or going through a foggy life situation, try to remember it's temporary.

You may need to take it slowly and cautiously. You may need to shine a different light into the fog.

You may need to pull over to the side for a while or take a pause to assess a situation. You will eventually move forward and continue your journey, on the road and in life.

25

PHONE-Y BEHAVIOR

Mobile phones. Two words that when put together have significantly changed civilization as we know it.

I look around. Everywhere I go, I see people buried in their phones. (Are they even called phones anymore?)

Age doesn't matter. I've seen five year olds use a cell phone like they were born with one in their hand. I've seen eighty year olds texting, reading email, and playing games on them. Race, creed, color of skin, ethnic or cultural background? Gather them up in a big ball and throw them out the window because a cell phone doesn't care about any of them. Wealthy, middle class, not so wealthy. Kick them to the curb. Just about everyone has a mobile device, from flip phones to tablets. There's a device for everyone! They gather up all of our info and habits and likes and dislikes and send them off into the netherworld to be used for us and against us. But I digress. That's a whole 'nother book.

Let me get back in my lane. Okay. I have to take a minute here. Breath, Rich. Breathe. (You can go grab a snack or take a quick power nap or go pee or whatever you feel like; I'm just gathering my thoughts about what to write next.)

Hey! Come back! I'm here now.

Now, take a mobile device and carry it with you into a vehicle.

Now put that vehicle into motion. You know what you have?

A lethal weapon!

(I am sure that after this chapter, I will never be able to make or get a call, send or get an email, play a game, or get online on my phone ever again. I'll also probably get thousands of spam texts and marketing calls every day, but it's a risk I am willing to take for the greater good!)

Yes, that's right. Take someone with a mobile device and put them behind the wheel of a moving vehicle, and you've just created a very dangerous recipe.

I am too lazy to look it up, so go online and see how many vehicular incidents, fatal and nonfatal, are caused per year by texting or talking while driving. (For God's sake, do not do it while you're driving!) I'll bet the numbers are mind-boggling. (What exactly is a boggle?)

Okay, okay. I looked it up. It took me two seconds.

The National Safety Council reports that cell phone use while driving leads to *1.6 million crashes each year.* Nearly 390 thousand injuries occur each year from accidents caused by texting while driving. In the United States, one out of every four car accidents is caused by texting while driving, with over 400 fatalities.

What else can be said?

Texting while driving is a selfish act and should never be done. Pull over! Try to think about others and how a couple of seconds of selfishness could alter your life and quite possibly other lives as well. This doesn't apply only to driving. Take a minute to ponder selfishness in general in your life.

I know I have usually not felt great after committing a selfish act.

Many of my selfish acts have caused direct or indirect harm to myself or others. Sometimes both. Selfishness is always motivated by fear—fear I don't have enough of something or fear I won't be recognized or validated.

I can almost always rationalize or justify my selfishness, and I've come to realize that anything I need to rationalize or justify is usually something that is not rational or justifiable. It usually means I am up to no good.

Now, is holding a cell phone to text, read email, or talk while driving a crime? *Yes*, it is! In some states, it carries a heavy fine and points on your driver's license. It can be injurious to yourself and others or even fatal.

Don't be selfish. Try to think of others. These are words to live life by.

Suggestion: Read this chapter until it sinks in.

26

DUI OR DON'T I?

Throughout the writing of this book, I wrestled with whether or not I should include this chapter. I finally decided it is impossible to sweep an elephant under a rug, so here it is.

Imagine picking up a gun and loading it with one bullet. You put the gun up to your head and pull the trigger. Click. Nothing happens. You then point the gun at another person. Click. Nothing happens. You keep pointing the gun at another person, then another, and another. Pointing and clicking. Eventually, if you keep pulling the trigger, that bullet is going to explode out of the chamber and find its target, either injuring or killing that unfortunate person.

I've just described what happens every time someone gets behind the wheel of a vehicle and drives under the influence of alcohol or drugs. Is this an extreme metaphor? I think not.

Every day, I read, hear, or see something about someone being killed or injured by a driver who was under the influence. Every single day.

I grew up in the 1960s and -0s. Alcohol and drugs flowed freely. Back then, I was pulled over many times while under the influence and was told to sleep it off until I was able to drive. That, or I was actually followed home and watched as my car was safely parked. I was never arrested or even issued a summons. I thank the universe every day that I didn't kill or injure myself or others. This would never happen today because there is zero tolerance for driving under the influence (and rightfully so!).

Today, there are no excuses for driving when one shouldn't be. Designated drivers. Ride shares. Taxis. Public transportation. There are even some services that will provide a driver who will come and pick up you and your car and drive it home for you.

Restaurants and bars can now be held responsible by law for allowing someone to leave their premises in a condition that is not conducive to driving. (Nothing helps to enforce the law like liability.) You get the drift.

DUI or DWI are entirely selfish acts.

Doing either is a total disregard for the well-being of oneself and others. It's an act of insanity. It is carelessness to the extreme. It is selfishness maximized.

I have seen lives changed forever in a split second by a drunk or drugged-up driver. Guilt, shame, resentment, denial, anger, and remorse are all wrapped up in a neat little package just waiting to be opened.

It's the gift that never stops giving to whomever gives it and whomever receives it.

One does not have to be an addict or an alcoholic to drive while impaired. (Although the odds increase dramatically if one is.) It can happen to anyone. It just takes one moment or one bad decision, and bang, you're in it.

If you are an addict or an alcoholic, I implore you to seek treatment or at the very least not to drive while drunk or impaired. There is no rationalization or self-justification for doing so. There are many spiritual and medical paths you can take to achieve sobriety. There are books, videos, programs, and podcasts galore. There is a very well-known fellowship with millions of people that has helped so many addicts to recover. There is no shame in seeking recovery from addiction. If you're a social drinker, please do not let one drunken or drugged-up moment shape the rest of your life and possibly others' lives. People die or are seriously injured every day by a drunk or impaired driver who considered themselves to be a normal, average, otherwise law-abiding human (whatever your definition of normal or average or law-abiding is!). I could go on and on. I could write another book entirely on this subject, but for now I am choosing to include it as a brief chapter in this book.

This is a very real problem in our society. It knows no race, creed, social status, financial condition, or gender— it affects all of them. Please make a conscious choice not to contribute to it.

Suggestion: Don't drive drunk or impaired. Period.

If you find yourself in a vehicle and you are impaired and about to turn the key, please pause and then play the movie to the end. Think about the worst thing that could happen because it actually could happen.

Call a cab, a ride share, or a sober friend. Do not drive. Save your life. Save someone else's life.

Conclusion

I think I have pretty much covered everything I could think of that relates to the way I drive reflecting the way I think and live my life. If I have missed anything, please feel free to scribble your additions in the margins or in any other blank spots on these pages.

I hope you have been able to identify with some or all of the thoughts and feelings I have expressed. I like the thought of taking whatever resonates with you and leaving whatever doesn't. I still have a way to go on my journey, and I would love to say I practice everything in this book to the letter, but I'm guessing that like you, I am still a work in progress and I most likely will be until I leave this beautiful planet. It's really all about the journey and the way I choose to experience it. The way I think becomes the way I live, and that becomes what my life looks like: love or fear.

Please try be kind to the other drivers on the road. Try to think of them as part of the whole, just like you and me. Imagine you are on the other end of your angry, fearful thoughts because you actually are. Our brothers and sisters are our biggest mirrors, reflecting back at us what we are showing them. Likewise, you are on the other end of your loving and kind thoughts. Doing unto others is really doing unto yourself because we are all part of the one. Drive safely. Remember that your vehicle is not a weapon unless you choose to turn it into one. Whatever you are doing on the inside of your vehicle will show on the outside in some way, so I suggest you choose lovingly and considerately.

May you have a comfortable and peaceful journey as you travel the highways and byways of destiny. May your road be smooth and beautifully landscaped. Enjoy the journey because eventually we will all wind up at the same destination.

With love and light,
Richie

Angry Driver Checklist

Check all that apply to you.

( ) I will tailgate the car ahead of me like a race-car driver drafting and slingshotting if it is not going as fast as I think it should, even though I have plenty of room to go around it.

( ) My high beams are used for more than just dark roads (flashing the car ahead of me that just won't get out of my way).

( ) My hands frequently hurt from gripping the steering wheel too hard out of anger or frustration with all of the idiots who have the nerve to be on the road at the exact same time as me. (Don't they realize I have to be somewhere?)

( ) My hands frequently hurt from pounding on the dashboard or steering wheel for a reason other than keeping the beat with that kick-ass *blank* song. (You can shout out whatever band floats your boat!)

( ) My voice is very hoarse from screaming at the car six lengths ahead of me for cutting into the lane I am speeding in and slowing me down by three miles per hour.

( ) I feel that at least one if not all of the other drivers woke up today with the express intention of sticking it to me every chance they could get.

( ) I fantasize about having high-powered lasers in my front and rear bumpers that could zero in on and melt any part of any vehicle ahead of or behind me—tires, taillights, vanity plates, etc.

( ) I imagine what it would be like to have titanium brush guards on the front of my vehicle for the purpose of "head butting" any vehicle impudent enough to do anything that I find offensive—cutting me off, going too slow, changing into my lane without signaling, etc.

( ) I believe the word *mobile* in mobile phone means it was meant to be used predominantly in an auto*mobile.*

( ) I believe a yellow traffic light means "speed up now."

( ) I believe that a stop sign doesn't have to be taken literally and that I can kind of just pause at it long enough to look both ways.

( ) I have invented whole new profanity-laced sentences to describe the other drivers on the road. This book is G rated, so you will have to use your imagination.

( ) When I get to my destination and exit my vehicle, I feel like I am returning from battle and that I have once again emerged victoriously.

( ) When I get to my destination and exit my vehicle, I feel like I am returning from battle and that I have once again emerged defeated.

( ) I believe the bigger and more powerful my vehicle is, the bigger and more powerful I am.

( ) I believe the smaller and less powerful my vehicle is, the bigger and more powerful I am. (Think about this one for a minute.)

If you have checked one to three boxes, you have an angry driver personality. If you have checked four to seven boxes, you have a really, really angry driver personality. If you have checked more than seven boxes, you should immediately seek psychiatric help because we may soon see your name next to something you really don't want to see your name next to on Google.

Disclaimer: This checklist has not been sanctioned or endorsed by any mental health professional or organization. You cannot use the results as an excuse to call out of work, collect any government funds, or to just be an all-around butthole.

Printed in the United States
by Baker & Taylor Publisher Services